BETWEEN
THE
STRIPES

BETWEEN
THE
STRIPES

A LEADER'S
PLAYBOOK
FOR
EARNING
YOUR
STRIPES
PART II

DR. JOHN LAURIE

authorHOUSE®

AuthorHouse™ LLC
1663 Liberty Drive
Bloomington, IN 47403
www.authorhouse.com
Phone: 1-800-839-8640

Published by AuthorHouse   08/12/2013

ISBN: 978-1-4918-0027-0 (sc)
ISBN: 978-1-4918-0028-7 (hc)
ISBN: 978-1-4918-0029-4 (e)

Library of Congress Control Number: 2013913470

INTRODUCTION

BETWEEN THE STRIPES:
A LEADER'S PLAYBOOK
FOR EARNING YOUR STRIPES PART II

This book has obviously been written for those who officiate, umpire, referee and judge sporting events. It has also been purposely designed for leaders in business, other professions and avocations to encourage "thinking outside the box" while establishing, reviewing or modifying their philosophy of leadership. If you look at this book only as through the eyes of a sports official, the "covers" may be too far apart . . . so read between the lines!

Hopefully this book will help trap you into doing your own thinking for developing, re-thinking or re-framing your own leadership style. In other words, the author is challenging you to personalize your own style of leadership and make it work for you. The author also believes that many of you will be more focused in your philosophy of leadership and rewarded if you apply some of these thoughts and concepts to your own life style.

For the officials who read this book, a special suggestion! This book should be reviewed (for sure) three times during your career: at the beginning, the middle and the end. The opportunity to reflect on these thoughts will present a different perspective each time around. For sports officials, it will enhance your concepts of what the best officials and crew leaders do in order to be successful.

There really wasn't much to writing this book! All the author had to do was think of every good and bad game, every good and poor game officiated that he was a part of or had observed over the past forty years and sit down at a computer. Another way to look at it is that you are not paying for this book as the author did but only the cost of the printing!

The author would like to answer the question that some may ask regarding why he used the format of quotations to present his point of view. As a former school teacher, coach, official, school administrator and professor for over forty years, he observed the power of using quotations to communicate in the school house and on the football field was very effective in motivating people.

For over thirty years the author has collected quotations from a wide variety of sources including books, newspapers, radio, TV, movies, Internet, clinics, conferences, casual conversations, and any other place one could find pithy expressions that could be transformed into insightful and/or provocative thoughts about leadership and sports officials.

The author found quotations to be a powerful tool to motivate his football crews individually and collectively, to improve their expectations, to set goals and become more effective officials. It will become very obvious to the readers that the author's comments will not tell you something you don't already know, but hopefully will broaden your scope of understanding some of the concepts of leadership and officiating shared in this book. I also realize that many of these quotations would be much more believed if you were told Ben Franklin said it first!

This book represents the fourth in a series written in this format style. The first is MANAGING THE GAME, the second is BETWEEN THE STRIPES: ZANY ZEBRA ZINGERS and the third is BETWEEN THE STRIPES: A LEADER'S PLAYBOOK FOR EARNING YOUR STRIPES PART I. The author has also published a book with over seventy stories about his officiating career in the Big 8 and Bit XII Football Conference titled WHY I DON'T BOO OFFICIALS.

DEDICATION

RED CASHION: Fired from the Southwest and Southland Conferences before working for the NFL for over 40 years!

From this dubious beginning, Red continued to pursue his dream with perseverance, dedication and talent until one day he was inducted into the Texas Sports Hall of Fame, officiated three Super Bowls, was described as "the most well known NFL official in history" and is the only official to be named to the All-Madden Team.

It is with great pleasure and humility that I dedicate this book to my friend and officiating mentor, Red Cashion. Our paths crossed while I was officiating in the Big XII Conference where I was a referee and he was an observer.

He was always friendly and gracious but he had no idea how much his professional comportment observed on television, or his comments at our clinics, would influence my officiating career as a referee.

Recently I asked Red to review material that appears in this book. His very positive response to the content has inspired me to continue my efforts to complete other book topics: Pregame, Poor Officiating and Supervisors and Observers.

Red and my wife Connie were also instrumental in encouraging me to select quotations from all four books I have written and package them as "Flash Cards" to improve officiating, which will be available July 2013.

SPECIAL RECOGNITION

My wife and I would like to especially recognize two very good football players that have played a significant role in our lives "off" of the football field.

My brother, Dave Laurie, was a tremendous high school football player at Atchison High School (Kansas) and then went on to start at Kansas State University playing the positions of linebacker, running back and kicker for the Wildcats. Although my brother, Phil, and I have teased him, we have not given him enough credit for his career as a high school football official. He was an excellent high school football official and part of a great crew that was well respected in the Central Kansas area where he officiated for several years.

He was an exemplary Professor at Kansas State University and recognized for his academic work at Oklahoma State University and K.S.U. in the areas of Health Education, Physical Education and Library Media Technology. He is most proud to have been recognized as "Outstanding Professor" by the student body at K.S.U.

Dave is also well-known around the United States for his collection of antique cars and his earlier work with the Fellowship of Christian Athletes.

Dr. Laurie has been married to his beautiful wife, Claudette, for 50 years. They have three children: Mark, Matt and Mike and five grandchildren: Jake, Alex, Megan, Brett and Hazel!

I am very proud of you, Bro!

Keith Finlayson is also in the category of being an excellent high school football player, playing both offense and defense for the Trojans in Carrollton, MO, with linebacker being his chosen slot. He was notorious among our conference and district schools, respected by players and a favorite of the coaches for his talent and knowledge of the game, as well as his toughness and the enthusiasm with which he played.

The pride and joy that Keith gave me as his mother are not only from sharing his football experience but from lessons that these years instilled in him . . . leadership, teamwork, loyalty, sportsmanship and the desire to walk off the field having given his all. These are the qualities that have helped mold him into the man he is today.

After graduating from the University of Arkansas, Keith worked in management for eighteen years, owned and operated own business for 7 years and still enjoys his avocation as a scuba instructor at highest level of education. After earning his M.S. while living in Chicago, Illinois, Keith taught in the Kankakee

Dr. John Laurie

school system, also coaching football and wrestling. Ten years ago he returned to Carrollton as the Technology Director, head wrestling coach and assistant football coach for the Carrollton R VII School District. He currently resides there with his wife, Susan.

His strength and courage have been a mainstay for his family in both good and tough times. He is "my shining star!"

Connie Laurie

ACKNOWLEDGMENT

CONNIE AND I AT A BOOK SIGNING IN MANHATTAN, KANSAS

One of the special benefits of making a book together is the opportunity to go out and meet old friends and make new ones. It has given us the chance to work on a project together as well as to travel to a number of states, enjoying the scenery and being in many wonderful book stores.

I have dedicated previous books to my mother and father, family members and deceased officials. This book is dedicated to all of those officials at the high school, college, university and N.F.L. level who have completed their careers performing at their very best.

Dr. John Laurie

It is a tribute to the individual officials and crews that have demonstrated throughout their careers, high leadership and exemplary officiating. I would also like to dedicate this book to those officials on their way to becoming the very best officials at their chosen level of officiating.

A very special thank you to my wife Connie, for her suggestions, encouragement and formatting this book for publication. Also my thanks to Steve Thomas, Creative Design Art Director, Camp David, Overland Park, Kansas for the cover design of this book and the other four that I have published.

JCL

ENDORSEMENTS

RED CASHION, REFEREE N.F.L., RETIRED: "You have done a wonderful job of providing assistance to all officials at every level. Your use of the relationship between official and coach is wonderful. I have always felt WE NEEDED to do a better job of making the coach think we are looking out for him.

John, I have always admired your work both on and off the field and the way you try to educate those associated with you. That education is without question one of the biggest responsibilities we have as referees. You do it so well. Working with you on material shows me how close our philosophies are about the work we do on and off the field.

I think in addition to this book, you should make these quotations into flash cards that every official could carry with him and use to get ready for the game. I always felt that mental preparation for an official at the time of the game is vital to a good game. In the few minutes before we went onto the field, I liked to ask my cohorts to tell me something that could happen on the kickoff or something like that just to make sure they were thinking football. You have done a wonderful job of providing that assistance to any official.

(I responded to Red's suggestion by creating REF-DECKS: 7 sets of 150 coated cards, 300 quotations in each set, a total of 2100 statements on these topics: Good Officials, Best Crews, Leadership, Communications/Coaches, Rookies & Mistakes, Supervisors & Observers, Pregame & Mechanics. For more information contact the author at johnclaurie@yahoo.com)

TOM OSBORNE, ATHLETIC DIRECTOR EMERITUS, FORMER HEAD COACH, UNIVERSITY OF NEBRASKA: "I have known John Laurie for many years when I was coaching at the University of Nebraska and John was an official in the Big 8 Conference and later the Big XII Conference. John was always a very accomplished and accurate official. His book BETWEEN THE STRIPES: A LEADER'S PLAYBOOK FOR EARNING YOUR STRIPES is an excellent handbook full of wisdom for those who are interested in officiating. I recommend it highly."

ED HOCHULI, N.F.L. REFEREE: "Your book is full of great philosophies, John. I love the sound of them. You've laid out several catchy phrases that are right on point and the way you have worded them really hits you and sticks with you. Congratulations and best of luck with the book."

COACH BILL SNYDER, KANSAS STATE UNIVERSITY: "John, a truly unique format which allows one to truly focus on each concept. Certainly many significant and helpful thoughts for coaches as well as officials and, if we think a little deeper, we may find many vital principles of life."

DICK HONIG, BIG 10 REFEREE, PRESIDENT OF HONIG'S WHISTLE STOP: "This book would be an excellent resource for anyone that officiates. It is geared to the football official but the contents are applicable to all sports. This book offers the insight and philosophies that will be very helpful to the new official, while at the same time serving as a reminder to the successful official of how he got there and what it takes to remain on top. This is a GOOD book . . ."

COACH MAC BROWN, UNIVERSITY OF TEXAS, FOOTBALL: "I enjoyed reading your comments and one-liners about officiating. You have always been seen as a first-class official and a friend. Thank you for your amazing contributions over a long period of time."

BILL CAROLLO, N.F.L. REFEREE (RETIRED), SUPERVISOR OF OFFICIALS FOR THE BIG 10 CONFERENCE, MID AMERICA CONFERENCE AND MISSOURI VALLEY CONFERENCE: "I always enjoy reading your work. Congratulations on your new book."

MIKE BURTON, SUPERVISOR GNAC AND NWC FOR FOOTBALL: "I enjoyed reading the sayings. A number of the sayings go along with the view that I have formulated after working with high school and college officials. A weak official never remembers his errors; a strong official never forgets his. Just like an official reviewing his keys before each game for each situation, these are good sayings to think about during your career. All the best with your book."

JOHN MACKOVIC, FORMER FOOTBALL COACH OF THE K.C. CHIEFS AND UNIVERSITY OF TEXAS: "You have found a fortunate method to tell your stories and I thoroughly enjoy the wit and humor. I think people will enjoy reading it."

BILLY ALTON, WVIAC FOOTBALL SUPERVISOR: "Having been a player, an assistant coach, a head coach, an official, a supervisor and now a TA in two DIVISION I leagues, I feel this book should be required reading for any official working college football. You have defined officiating in simplistic terms: relationships between the group and relationships between officials and coaches. These simplistic statements should allow officials to work with six other individuals in a very cohesive manner."

BILL HANCOCK, EXECUTIVE DIRECTOR OF BOWL CHAMPIONSHIP SERIES (BCS), FORMER ASSISTANT COMMISSIONER, BIG 8 CONFERENCE: "Congratulations on the completion of this book. The draft looks great and I look forward to purchasing a copy. I will talk it up among my colleagues. As you probably remember, I love and respect officials. Many of my best memories are about the great times I enjoyed with the men who administered the games."

BILL SCHMITZ, BIG 8, NFL (RETIRED): "I can remember when I first began my officiating career that our referee, Jack Baker, had a book of sayings that he would bring along to our games and read a few to us at the end of our pregame. I can't really remember what the effect was at the time, but I remember them now. Maybe they did make an impression on me.

I can see officials benefiting from the wisdom of your book. I can also appreciate the flexibility of the book being able to move into anyone's world by merely changing "referee, official" to management, labor, salesman customer, principal, teacher, etc. I hope that you have a good marketing program because I believe that these adages will be very effective to those zebras."

PHIL LAURIE, MIAA FOOTBALL SUPERVISOR, BIG 8 OFFICIAL, BIG XII OFFICIAL AND OBSERVER: "What do I look for when selecting officials for my staff? I believe if you read this book and select five to ten of these quotes and make them part of your game to game officiating ritual, you will become a great crewmate. You will see what the great officials do to get to the top."

BRAD VAN VARK, REFEREE BIG XII CONFERENCE: "As the referee in my first Division I game and a few others to follow, I am very grateful to the start you helped provide me in officiating Division I football. I am a proud owner of one of your other books and it is interesting to review those books throughout my progression in officiating and see the different perspectives I have now from way back when.

As I start a new journey as a Referee, I would love to purchase your new book to help myself, my crew and my sales people at Pella. I report to a VP at Pella who is also a big fan of quotations to help motivate and provoke thoughts among our team. I plan to let him borrow it from time to time to grab a few ideas for his use."

MIKE WEATHERFORD, BIG XII, N.F.L. OFFICIAL "Whenever I was assigned with John Laurie I always looked forward to it. I knew we would have some thought-provoking quotes to review. We wouldn't complicate the game with mismanagement, and if we threw a flag, the call should call itself. No nickel and dime calls, only Super Bowl calls! This is what he related to his crew. He set the tone; the rest of the crew followed."

MIKE GOTTFRIED, UNIVERSITY OF KANSAS FOOTBALL COACH (RETIRED): "I found your book to be full of leadership and teamwork concepts that go far beyond the football field. I would include business men/women and even the support of family values to be reviewed in this book. I can without reservation recommend it for officials, coaches, players, fans and business leaders as a "gut check" for what is important. And John, you and your brother (Frank and Jesse)* were outstanding college officials. I found many of your qualities outlined in this book." *Inside joke (☺)

ABOUT THE AUTHOR

John Laurie, Ph.D. has been an educator for 40 years. He has been recognized as an innovative high school principal in Topeka, Kansas; Springfield, Missouri; Shawnee Mission, Kansas, and Blue Valley, Overland Park, Kansas. He was also an Associate Professor at Emporia State University, Emporia, Kansas and Baker University, Baldwin, Kansas. He is presently retired.

He was honored as "Missouri High School Principal of the Year" and received the "Alumni Fellow Award from the College of Education" from Kansas State University. Laurie received his B.S. and Ph.D. degrees from Kansas State University and his Masters Degree from the University of Colorado.

He developed a block schedule for high schools that is used in over 4000 schools (The Hillcrest Plan), as well as many of our department of Defense Schools worldwide. He has presented on this topic in 37 states and in Panama, Japan, Belgium, Australia and Germany.

His officiating career spans over 40 years. He has officiated Kansas state high school football and basketball championships at every level. Laurie officiated small college football and basketball for over 20 years. He was a referee in the Big 8 Conference for 13 years, 11 years in the Big XII Conference and Replay Official for the Big XII Conference for three years. He was also president of both Big 8 and Big XII Football Associations. Laurie officiated as a referee at numerous conference championships as well as the following Bowl games:

> Rose Bowl (2), Sugar Bowl, Fiesta Bowl, Peach Bowl (2), Coca-Cola Bowl (Japan), Sun Bowl, Cotton Bowl, Aloha Bowl and Mobile Bowl.

He is also the author of the following books: MANAGING THE GAME, WHY I DON'T BOO OFFICIALS, BETWEEN THE STRIPES: ZANY ZEBRA ZINGERS and BETWEEN THE STRIPES: A LEADER'S PLAYBOOK FOR EARNING YOUR STRIPES PART I and PART II.

THE "AUTHORITY" FOR BEING THE REFEREE IS A POOR SUBSTITUTE FOR LEADERSHIP.

JOHN C LAURIE

THERE ARE SOME PROBLEMS IN A GAME IN WHICH THERE ARE SIMPLY NO SOLUTIONS. THE KEY IS COPING WITH THE PROBLEMS USING COMMON SENSE AND NOT MAKING THE MISTAKE OF CREATING BIGGER PROBLEMS.

A GOOD QUALITY FOR THE REFEREE AFTER THE GAME IS TO FIND SOMETHING THAT EACH CREW MEMBER DID RIGHT AND TELL HIM.

JOHN C LAURIE

THE BEST CREWS FIND WAYS TO DO THE LITTLE THINGS RIGHT WHICH CAUSE ALL OF THE "BIG THINGS" TO HAVE A RHYTHM OF ORDER AND FAIRNESS WHEN THEY OCCUR.

OFFICIALS WITH THE MOST SKILL HAVE
THE ABILITY TO CONCEAL THEIR SKILL.

JOHN C LAURIE

GENERALLY THE LEAST CONVERSATION
YOU CAN HAVE WITH A COACH DURING
AN EMOTIONAL TIME IS IF THE END IS
CLOSE TO THE BEGINNING.

THE BEST OFFICIALS ARE NEVER SATISFIED WHEN SATISFACTION BECOMES CONVENIENT AND THE NORM.

> JOHN C LAURIE

GOOD OFFICIALS ARE VERY AWARE THAT EVERY TIME YOU BLOW YOUR WHISTLE OR THROW YOUR FLAG SOMEONE WILL BELIEVE YOU WERE WRONG.

AVERAGE OFFICIALS LEARN FROM OTHERS. GOOD OFFICIALS LEARN FROM THE RULEBOOK. THE BEST ONES LEARN FROM THEIR MISTAKES.

JOHN C LAURIE

THE EMPHASIS DURING A TOUGH CRISIS ON THE FIELD MUST BE, "WHAT'S WRONG AND HOW DO WE CORRECT IT?" NOT "WHO'S TO BLAME FOR THIS MESS?"

YOUR FUTURE REPUTATION AS AN
OFFICIAL IS A RECORD OF THE PAST.

JOHN C LAURIE

IF YOUR GOAL IS TO BE A BETTER
OFFICIAL THAN ANYONE ELSE, THE ONLY
WAY YOU CAN GO IS "DOWN" AFTER
THAT. A BETTER GOAL IS TO SEEK TO BE A
LITTLE BETTER EACH GAME.

IF YOU GET "LOST" IN A COMPLICATED
SITUATION AND NEED ASSISTANCE
FROM THE CREW, BE CAREFUL WHO YOU
BORROW FROM.

JOHN C LAURIE

A REFEREE CAN'T COMPROMISE HIS
PRINCIPLES, BUT HE CAN COORDINATE
TACTICS TO PRESERVE UNITY WITHIN
THE CREW.

GOOD OFFICIALS TRY TO CORRECT THEMSELVES SO OTHERS WON'T HAVE TO,

JOHN C LAURIE

THE CHEMISTRY BETWEEN THE REFEREE AND THE CREW IS VERY IMPORTANT AS EACH CREW MEMBER NEEDS TO KNOW WHAT HE STANDS FOR—AS WELL AS WHAT HE WON'T STAND FOR.

REPUTATION IS A GOOD BAROMETER BUT CHARACTER IS THE BEST MEASURE OF AN OFFICIAL'S CAREER.

JOHN C LAURIE

YOUR REPUTATION FOR THE LENGTH OF YOUR CAREER CAN BE DETERMINED BY YOUR CONDUCT DURING A SINGLE DECISION OF ONE GAME.

STAYING ON THE RIGHT TRACK TO GET TO THE TOP MAY REQUIRE A DETOUR FROM TIME TO TIME.

JOHN C LAURIE

DISCRETION COMBINED WITH COMMON SENSE IS THE BEST ROUTE WHEN YOU DON'T HAVE A REMEDY FOR A SITUATION IN A DIFFICULT GAME.

THE BEST OFFICIALS HAVE THE ABILITY TO LAND ON THEIR FEET WHEN EVERYTHING ELSE IS TURNED UPSIDE DOWN.

JOHN C LAURIE

WE ALL KNOW A FOOLISH OFFICIAL WHEN WE SEE ONE. IF YOU ARE ON A GOOD CREW, THEY WILL TELL YOU WHEN YOU ARE ACTING LIKE ONE.

THE BEST OFFICIALS HAVE THE ABILITY
TO LOOK FORWARD WITH CONFIDENCE
AND BACKWARD WITH GRATITUDE.

JOHN C LAURIE

THE BEST OFFICIALS CAN SIMPLIFY
COMPLEX PLAYS; POOR OFFICIALS
HAVE A TENDENCY TO MAKE SIMPLE
SITUATIONS COMPLEX.

SOMETIMES IT IS NECESSARY FOR COMMON SENSE TO OVER-RULE RULES IN A FOOTBALL GAME.

JOHN C LAURIE

GOOD REFEREES BELIEVE ONLY HALF OF WHAT THEY HEAR FROM A COACH; THE BEST ALSO KNOW WHICH HALF THAT IS.

LEARN ALL YOU CAN LEARN FROM OTHER OFFICIALS, BUT KNOWING YOURSELF IS MORE IMPORTANT.

JOHN C LAURIE

ONE OF THE REAL CHALLENGES FOR A YOUNG OFFICIAL IS TO BE SUCCESSFUL ON A MEDIOCRE CREW. YOU MUST FIT IN WITHOUT BUYING IN.

NIGHTMARE GAMES CAN BE AVOIDED BY VISUALIZING AND PROJECTING THOUGHTS OF WELL-OFFICIATED GAMES.

JOHN C LAURIE

CAB DRIVERS ARE LIVING PROOF THAT PRACTICE DOES NOT MAKE PERFECT BUT PERFECT PRACTICE DOES MAKE GOOD OFFICIALS.

MOST VERY GOOD REFEREES WOULD
LIKE TO REPEAT THEIR CAREERS JUST
MAKING THEIR MISTAKES EARLIER.

JOHN C LAURIE

THE DIFFERENCE BETWEEN TAKING A
CALCULATED RISK AND MAKING A RASH
DECISION IS THE FINE LINE THAT DIVIDES
GOOD AND POOR OFFICIALS.

OFFICIATING SIMPLY BOILS DOWN TO BEING ONLY AS GOOD AS THE LAST GAME YOU OFFICIATED.

JOHN C LAURIE

THE REFEREE WITH THE BEST "STYLE" SHOULD BE LIKE HIS UNIFORM AND DRAW AS LITTLE ATTENTION TO HIMSELF AS POSSIBLE.

AN OFFICIAL BECOMES WISE AND MAKES IMPROVEMENT BY OBSERVING WHAT HAPPENS WHEN HE ISN'T.

JOHN C LAURIE

THE REFEREE NEEDS TO BE AWARE IF SOMEONE BRINGS HIM A SECOND OPINION THAT MAY BE EXACTLY HOW LONG IT WAS THOUGHT ABOUT.

PERSISTENCE IS STICKING TO OFFICIATING EFFECTIVELY A ONE-SIDED GAME SO THAT YOU DON'T GET STUCK.

JOHN C LAURIE

THE ULTIMATE TEST OF THE CHARACTER OF AN OFFICIAL IS HOW HE ACTS AFTER OFFICIATING THE POOREST GAME OF HIS CAREER.

THE ONLY TIME A GOOD CREW GETS IN THE WAY OF A CREW MEMBER IS IF HE IS HEADED DOWN.

JOHN C LAURIE

WISE OFFICIALS KNOW WHAT TO DO, SKILLED OFFICIALS KNOW HOW TO DO IT, AND THE BEST OFFICIALS FOLLOW THROUGH.

NOTHING COSTS MORE OF THE CREW LEADER THAN TO CARE ABOUT EACH MEMBER—EXCEPT NOT CARING.

JOHN C LAURIE

MANY TIMES DURING A DIFFICULT PART OF OFFICIATING A GAME, PATIENCE WILL ACHIEVE MORE THAN FORCE.

KNOWLEDGE OF RULES IS IMPORTANT BUT WISDOM AND EXPERIENCE IS EQUALLY VALUABLE.

JOHN C LAURIE

WHEN THE REFEREE USES HIS AUTHORITY LIKE A BANK ACCOUNT, THE MORE HE DRAWS ON IT THE LESS HE HAS.

AT LEAST SEVENTY-FIVE PERCENT OF OFFICIATING IMPROVEMENT COMES FROM THE ENCOURAGEMENT OF OTHERS.

JOHN C LAURIE

THERE IS A POINT IN EVERY GAME WHEN THE BEST WISDOM IS NOT TO CHANGE ANYTHING, BUT SIMPLY TO RE-ARRANGE THE SITUATION.

THE BEST CREWS SEE THROUGH EACH
OTHER AND STILL RESPECT EVERYONE
ON THE CREW.

JOHN C LAURIE

WHEN IT IS NECESSARY FOR YOU TO
TAKE A STAND WITH A COACH, MAKE
SURE YOUR FEET ARE ON THE GROUND
AND IN THE RIGHT PLACE.

OFFICIALS WHO GO "THE EXTRA MILE"
TO GET TO THE TOP NEVER FIND IT
CROWDED ALONG THE WAY.

JOHN C LAURIE

WHEN A COMPLEX SITUATION DEVELOPS
DURING A GAME, THE SIMPLEST
SOLUTION MAY NOT BE RIGHT BUT IT IS A
GOOD PLACE TO START.

THE REFEREE WHO IS SELF-CENTERED ALWAYS MAKES THOSE AROUND HIM UNCOMFORTABLE.

JOHN C LAURIE

THE CAPACITY FOR A CREW TO GET INTO TROUBLE OR TO GET OUT OF TROUBLE IS SELDOM THE PROPERTY OF THE SAME CREW.

ONE MEASURE OF A REFEREE'S
LEADERSHIP IS THE "SIZE" OF THE MEN
WHO WANT TO BE ON HIS CREW.

JOHN C LAURIE

POSITIVE THOUGHTS BY OFFICIALS
DURING A DIFFICULT GAME USUALLY
BRING POSITIVE ACTIONS BY PLAYERS
AND COACHES.

THE CREW CONCEPT OF "HAVING FUN"
IS A GOOD WAY TO TRAVEL BUT YOUR
GOAL AS A CREW IS TO OFFICIATE A
GREAT GAME.

JOHN C LAURIE

IF YOU ARE GOING TO AIM TO BE THE
BEST OFFICIAL AT YOUR POSITION, START
BUILDING YOUR AMMUNITION PILE.

FOR A CREW TO CLIMB TO THE TOP OF A GREASY POLE, THEY NEED TO BE WELL PREPARED FOR THE TRIP.

JOHN C LAURIE

A GAME IS NEVER SO ONE-SIDED OR POORLY PLAYED THAT YOUR COURTESY TO PLAYERS OR COACHES SHOULD BE COMPROMISED.

DON'T LET THE "RIGHT CALL" ON
THE FIELD PASS BECAUSE OF THE
INCONVENIENCE OF PERSONALLY
LOOKING BAD.

JOHN C LAURIE

KEEP PROBLEMS IN OFFICIATING A GAME
TO BITS IN BETWEEN LONG PERIODS
OF A GOOD FLOW OF A WELL-PLAYED/
OFFICIATED GAME.

WHAT IS ACTUALLY HAPPENING IN A
GAME IS SOMETIMES NOT AS IMPORTANT
AS WHAT APPEARS TO BE HAPPENING
OR COULD HAPPEN.

JOHN C LAURIE

SOMETIMES THE ONLY WAY WE CAN
DEVELOP GOOD JUDGMENT IS BY
EXPERIENCING BAD JUDGEMENT.

WHEN IT IS NOT NECESSARY TO THROW YOUR FLAG OR BLOW YOUR WHISTLE, IT IS NOT NECESSARY.

JOHN C LAURIE

AN OFFICIAL'S REPUTATION IS EARNED BY ACHIEVING AT HIS HIGHEST LEVEL TOWARDS SOMETHING THAT CAN'T BE DONE.

AN OFFICIAL WITH A GOOD MEMORY FORGETS THE RIGHT THING AT THE PROPER MOMENT.

JOHN C LAURIE

THE BEST WAY TO GET EVEN WITH ANOTHER CREW IS TO HELP THEM TO BECOME BETTER! YOU HAVE TAKEN THE HIGHER ROAD AND EVERYONE IMPROVES.

WHEN THERE IS A CRISIS ON THE FIELD, IT IS MUCH MORE DIFFICULT TO MAKE A MISTAKE WHEN YOU TAKE YOUR TIME.

JOHN C LAURIE

GOOD REFEREES INSPIRE THE CREW TO HAVE CONFIDENCE IN THEM; GREAT REFEREES INSPIRE CONFIDENCE IN EACH CREW MEMBER.

EXPERIENCED OFFICIALS RECOGNIZE
A MISTAKE BEFORE IT IS ABOUT TO
HAPPEN A SECOND TIME.

JOHN C LAURIE

THE GAME CLOCK IS THERE TO
KEEP THINGS FROM HAPPENING ALL AT
ONCE BUT IN SOME GAMES THAT IS NOT
THE CASE.

THE SMALL "BITS AND PIECES" OF A GAME EITHER FIT TOGETHER WITH A GOOD CREW OR BECOME TROUBLE FOR A POOR CREW.

JOHN C LAURIE

IT IS INTERESTING HOW MANY OFFICIALS BECOME VERY SUCCESSFUL WHO DID NOT HAVE THE ADVANTAGES OTHERS HAD.

THE BEST OFFICIALS HAVE THE ABILITY TO ANTICIPATE ALL OF THE CONSEQUENCES OF SITUATIONS ON THE FIELD.

JOHN C LAURIE

A GOOD REFEREE MAKING THE CORRECT DECISIONS IS VERY EFFECTIVE IN SORTING THROUGH THE NONESSENTIALS.

THE REAL MEASURE OF HOW EFFECTIVE AN OFFICIAL WAS DURING A GAME IS HOW MUCH BETTER HE MADE HIS CREW.

JOHN C LAURIE

THERE ARE CERTAIN TIMES IN A FOOTBALL GAME WHERE YOU ARE REQUIRED TO TRUST UNCERTAINTY TO BRING CLARITY TO THE SITUATION.

IT IS THE CAPACITY TO DEVELOP AND IMPROVE THEIR SKILLS THAT SEPARATES GOOD OFFICIALS FROM THE REST.

JOHN C LAURIE

MEMBERS OF THE BEST CREWS SHARE POSITIVE COMMENTS WITHIN THE CREW AND MAKE CONSTRUCTIVE COMMENTS TO EACH OTHER INDIVIDUALLY.

THE BEST WAY NOT TO SLIP UP DURING THE GAME IS TO STAY AWAY FROM SLIPPERY SITUATIONS.

JOHN C LAURIE

THE BEST OFFICIALS NEVER DO AS WELL IN THE GAME THAT JUST ENDED AS THEY PREPARE TO DO IN THE NEXT ONE.

WHEN THINGS START TO GO "SOUTH" IN A GAME, DON'T GO BACKWARDS WHEN YOU HAVE ALREADY BEEN THERE.

JOHN C LAURIE

A GOOD PREGAME CONFERENCE STARTS WITH "CREW" AND ENDS WITH THE LAST TWO LETTERS IN "PREGAME."

FAILURE BUILDS SUCCESS IF YOU ARE BEING YOURSELF AND NOT IMITATING ANOTHER OFFICIAL.

JOHN C LAURIE

THE BEST OFFICIALS ALWAYS ATTEMPT TO DO THEIR BEST. THE ONES AT THE VERY TOP ARE ABLE TO NOT ONLY DO THEIR BEST BUT WHAT IS REQUIRED.

BUILDING AN OFFICIATING CAREER IS IMPORTANT; MAINTAINING AND IMPROVING IT IS THE KEY.

JOHN C LAURIE

AFTER EACH GAME ASK, "AM I GETTING A LITTLE BETTER OR A LITTLE WORSE?" IF YOUR ANSWER IS THE SAME THREE GAMES IN A ROW, YOU ARE ON YOUR WAY.

SOME CREWS SEEM TO MAKE GAMES DIFFICULT; GOOD CREWS ALLOW DIFFICULT SITUATIONS TO DEFINE THEM.

JOHN C LAURIE

ONE OF THE BEST WAYS TO DESCRIBE A SUCCESSFUL OFFICIAL IS THAT HE HAS OVERCOME THE FEAR OF MAKING A MISTAKE.

GOOD OFFICIALS TAKE AS MUCH TIME
AS IT TAKES TO MAKE A SNAP CORRECT
DECISION.

JOHN C LAURIE

IF YOU OFFICIATE EVERY GAME WITH THE
EXCITEMENT OF YOUR FIRST GAME OR
THAT IT COULD BE YOUR LAST GAME, YOU
WILL APPRECIATE IT MUCH MORE.

THE CHOICES YOU MAKE AS A YOUNG OFFICIAL DETERMINE FUTURE CONSEQUENCES AND OPTIONS.

JOHN C LAURIE

THE FREQUENCY OF THE OCCURRENCE OF ERRORS IN A GAME IS INVERSELY PROPORTIONAL TO THEIR DESIRABILITY.

THE ONLY GOOD LUCK THAT GOOD CREWS HAVE IS THE ABILITY AND DEMONSTRATION TO OVERCOME BAD LUCK.

JOHN C LAURIE

THERE IS NO STRONGER BONDING EXPERIENCE FOR A CREW THAN TO SUCCESSFULLY WORK THROUGH DIFFICULT SITUATIONS TOGETHER AND OFFICIATE A GREAT GAME.

IF YOU STUMBLE ON THE PLAY DURING THE GAME, STAY FOCUSED AS IT MAY PREVENT A FALL.

JOHN C LAURIE

THE BEST OFFICIALS PUT RESPONSIBILITY ON THEIR SHOULDERS; POOR ONES KEEP A FEW CHIPS ON THEIR SHOULDERS.

THE BEST CREWS IN HIGH SCHOOL AND
COLLEGE FOOTBALL DO MORE THAN
THEIR ASSIGNED POSITIONS.

JOHN C LAURIE

IF YOU ARE THE BEST OFFICIAL IN
THE CONFERENCE AT YOUR POSITION,
YOU MUST WORK HARDER THAN THE
SECOND-BEST TO KEEP YOUR STATUS.

CONCENTRATION

The most important part of any pre-snap situation.

THE BEST OFFICIALS AND CREWS
HAVE THE ABILITY TO DEMONSTRATE
CONFIDENCE AT EASE.

JOHN C LAURIE

A GREAT GOAL FOR OFFICIALS IS TO
STRIVE TO ALLOW THE MISTAKES OF THE
PAST TO BE GREATER THAN ANY MADE IN
THE FUTURE.

THE BEST CREWS ACCEPT
DIFFICULT CIRCUMSTANCES AND
THEN SEEK APPROPRIATE ACTIONS TO
OVERCOME THEM.

JOHN C LAURIE

GREAT OFFICIALS ARE ALLOWED TO
HAVE A CAREFULLY SELECTED AREA OF
EXCESSIVENESS. THE KEY IS FINDING
ONE THAT DOES NOT DISTRACT FROM
THE GAME.

THE EASIEST WAY TO AVOID ERRORS
IN OFFICIATING IS TO CORRECT THEM
BEFORE THEY ARE IMPLEMENTED
BY RULE.

JOHN C LAURIE

DURING THE MOST STRESSFUL PART OF
DIFFICULT GAMES, THE BEST OFFICIALS
HAVE AN INTENSIFIED FEELING OF
NONCHALENCE.

THE MOST EXPERIENCED AND BEST OFFICIALS GIVE A LOT OF THOUGHT BEFORE MAKING SUDDEN DECISIONS.

JOHN C LAURIE

THE ONLY THING THE BEST ROOKIE OFFICIAL AND POOREST ROOKIE OFFICIAL HAVE IN COMMON IS THAT THEY STARTED THE SAME DAY.

IMPROVING OFFICIALS WILL LEARN FROM EACH SUCCESS AND EVEN MORE FROM EACH FAILURE.

JOHN C LAURIE

THE STRENGTH OF THE BEST CREWS INCREASES IN PROPORTION TO THE DIFFICULT SITUATIONS IN WHICH THEY ARE PLACED.

THE BEST OFFICIALS HAVE
A PRESENCE THAT IS STRONGER THAN
THEIR GREATEST WEAKNESS.

JOHN C LAURIE

YOU CAN ALWAYS TELL THE DIFFERENCE
BETWEEN A LUCKY CREW AND A GOOD
CREW BY THE DURATION OF THEIR
"LUCK TIME."

GOOD OFFICIALS WOULD ALWAYS
PREFER TO MAKE THEIR NAME IN
OFFICIATING THAN INHERIT IT.

JOHN C LAURIE

OFFICIALS NEED TO BE AWARE OF
LOGICAL CONSEQUENCES WHILE
KEEPING ALL OPTIONS OPEN AND
GETTING THE PLAY RESOLVED
CORRECTLY.

IT IS BETTER TO BE YOUR BEST AS AN
OFFICIAL THAN A SECOND COPY OF
SOMEONE ELSE'S BEST.

JOHN C LAURIE

WHEN YOU ARE ENDING A DIFFICULT
CONVERSATION WITH A COACH,
REMEMBER THAT THE END NEVER
JUSTIFIES MEANNESS.

ENTHUSIASM IS THE MOST IMPORTANT
QUALITY ANY OFFICIAL CAN BRING TO
THE CREW.

JOHN C LAURIE

THE BEST COMPLIMENT A REFEREE
COULD RECEIVE ABOUT HIS ROOKIE
CREW IS THAT HE PUT EXPERIENCED
HEADS ON YOUNG SHOULDERS.

MECHANICS AND ROUTINES CAN BE GOOD OR BAD DEPENDING ON WHETHER THEY ARE GOOD OR BAD HABITS.

JOHN C LAURIE

A CREW DOESN'T CARE HOW MUCH THE REFEREE KNOWS ABOUT FOOTBALL UNTIL THEY UNDERSTAND HOW MUCH HE CARES ABOUT THEM.

OFFICIALS TRUE TO THE CREW DON'T GET IN YOUR WAY EXCEPT TO KEEP YOU FROM GOING DOWN.

JOHN C LAURIE

SOME OF THE BEST OPPORTUNITIES TO DEMONSTRATE YOUR LEADERSHIP AS AN OFFICIAL ARE DISGUISED AS PROBLEMS.

POOR OFFICIALS OFFICIATE TO BE NOTICED; THE BEST OFFICIAL'S GOAL IS TO REMAIN UNNOTICED.

JOHN C LAURIE

SETTLE AN AWKWARD SITUATION EARLY IN THE GAME AND YOU WILL PREVENT SEVERAL DIFFICULT PROBLEMS IN THE LAST QUARTER.

GOOD OFFICIALS KNOW HOW BEST TO
DO IT WHILE EXEMPLARY OFFICIALS
KNOW WHAT IS BEST TO DO.

JOHN C LAURIE

THE BEST REFEREES DON'T SEE
THROUGH CREW MEMBERS, BUT HELP
TO SEE EACH OF THEM THROUGH
DIFFICULT SITUATIONS.

THE DIFFERENCE BETWEEN AN ORDINARY AND AN EXTRAORDINARY OFFICIAL IS SIMPLY A LITTLE EXTRA.

JOHN C LAURIE

THE BEST COMMUNICATING REFEREE HAS THE ABILITY TO SAY TO THE COACH ONLY WHAT HE WANTS HIM TO REMEMBER.

THE SECRET OF SUCCESS FOR ANY OFFICIAL IS TO DO THE COMMON THINGS UNCOMMONLY WELL.

JOHN C LAURIE

WHETHER YOU TAKE THE "EASY ROAD" OR EARN YOUR WAY TO THE TOP, THE RESULT IS STILL THE SAME . . . CONSEQUENCES.

THE BEST WAY TO HANDLE YOUR DISAPPOINTMENTS IN OFFICIATING IS TO CELEBRATE THE SUCCESSES OF OTHERS.

JOHN C LAURIE

THE BEST WAY FOR AN OFFICIAL TO IMPROVE HIS SELF-CONFIDENCE IS TO OVER-PREPARE.

AN OFFICIAL MAY BE BETTER THAN HIS REPUTATION, BUT NEVER BETTER THAN THE PRINCIPLES HE FOLLOWS.

JOHN C LAURIE

IN ORDER TO ADVANCE IN OFFICIATING, YOU MUST MAKE MORE OPPORTUNITIES THAN YOU FIND.

SOMETIMES THE BEST HELPING HAND YOU CAN GIVE A ROOKIE OFFICIAL IS A PUSH IN THE BACK.

JOHN C LAURIE

THE FIRST STEP TOWARDS PROFITING FROM OUR MISTAKE IS NOT TO BLAME OTHERS FOR IT.

EXCELLENCE IN OFFICIATING IS A RESULT OF DEDICATION TO WEEKLY PROGRESS THROUGHOUT THE SEASON.

JOHN C LAURIE

OFFICIALS WHO HAVE THE ABILITY TO GRACEFULLY ACKNOWLEDGE THEIR ERRORS AND NOT REPEAT THEM WILL ALWAYS PREVAIL.

NINETY PERCENT OF THE DELIGHT IN OFFICIATING A GREAT GAME IS TO KNOW IT AT THE TIME.

JOHN C LAURIE

A GOOD REMINDER FOR THE ROOKIE IN THE CREW IS "NOT TO DROWN THE CREW MEMBER WHO TAUGHT YOU HOW TO SWIM."

THE BRIGHTEST BULB ON THE CREW IS NOT AS EFFECTIVE AS THE OFFICIAL WITH CONSISTENT COMMON SENSE.

JOHN C LAURIE

THE MARK OF A GOOD SUPERVISOR, OFFICIAL OR CREW IS NOT TO BE SURPRISED BY ANYTHING THAT HAPPENS DURING THE GAME.

THERE MAY BE SOME LUCK IN BEING PERCEIVED AS A GOOD OFFICIAL BUT IT IS NOT LUCK IF YOU STAY THERE.

JOHN C LAURIE

A GOOD OFFICIAL WILL ONLY BELIEVE HALF OF WHAT A COACH TELLS HIM; THE BEST OFFICIAL CAN DISCERN WHICH HALF.

A ROOKIE OFFICIAL BELIEVES HE OFFICIATED A GOOD GAME AND AN EXPERIENCED OFFICIAL KNOWS.

JOHN C LAURIE

THE BEST CREWS HAVE THE ABILITY NOT ONLY TO OBSERVE THE UNUSUAL THINGS THAT OCCUR IN A GAME BUT ALSO THE OBVIOUS.

A ROOKIE OFFICIAL LOOKS FOR COMPLIMENTS; THE SEASONED OFFICIAL LOOKS FOR EVIDENCE OF EFFECTIVENESS.

JOHN C LAURIE

YOUR THOUGHT IN THE PREGAME DISCUSSION IS A REHEARSAL FOR PERFORMANCE DURING THE GAME.

THE BEST ADVICE FOR A NEW OFFICIAL IS TO BE SELECTIVE FROM WHOM YOU TAKE ADVICE.

JOHN C LAURIE

THE BEST OFFICIALS CONTROL THE DIFFICULT PARTS OF A GAME BY NOT MOVING WITH THE PROBLEMS BUT AHEAD OF THEM.

THE BEST OFFICIALS DEVELOP CONFIDENCE AND HAVE THE ABILITY TO KEEP IT FROM BECOMING CONCEIT.

JOHN C LAURIE

THE BEST OFFICIALS HAVE THE ABILITY TO CONSISTENTLY ANTICIPATE CONSEQUENCES AND MAKE THE CORRECT DECISION.

IF YOU ARE IN A POOR CREW, REDUCE YOUR EXPECTATIONS TO ZERO AND EXPECT A SERIES OF HAPPY SURPRISES.

JOHN C LAURIE

EVEN POOR OFFICIALS CAN TAKE AIM ON MAKING A DIFFICULT DECISION BUT ONLY THE GOOD ONES KNOW WHEN TO PULL THE TRIGGER.

THE SECRET OF BECOMING A SUCCESSFUL OFFICIAL IS TO HANG AROUND UNTIL YOU GET USED TO DOING IT.

JOHN C LAURIE

ONLY OFFICIALS OF THE HIGHEST CHARACTER CAN SUCCESSFULLY WITHSTAND THE ASSAULTS OF ENVY FROM OTHER OFFICIALS.

CREWS DON'T CHANGE TO IMPROVE;
INDIVIDUALS WITHIN THE CREW CHANGE
TO IMPROVE THE CREW.

JOHN C LAURIE

TOO MANY OFFICIALS NEVER REALIZE
UNTIL IT IS TOO LATE THAT THE REAL JOY
OF OFFICIATING IS TO ENJOY IT AT THAT
EXACT MOMENT!

CREW MORALE WILL IMPROVE WHEN YOU RAISE THE SELF-ESTEEM OF YOUR CREW MEMBERS.

JOHN C LAURIE

ALL GOOD OFFICIALS HAVE THREE "M'S":
- RIGHT MOVES,
- RIGHT MOMENT,
- RIGHT MOTIVE.

EXPERIENCED CREW OFFICIALS ARE
THE BONES THAT ROOKIE OFFICIALS
SHARPEN THEIR TEETH ON.

JOHN C LAURIE

EVERY OFFICIAL IN THE CREW CARRIES
THE BATON OF THE CONFERENCE AND
THE SUPERVISOR WHEN HE PUTS ON
HIS UNIFORM.

THE BEST WAY TO OBSERVE SEVERAL THINGS HAPPENING AT ONCE ON THE FOOTBALL FIELD IS ONE PART AT A TIME.

JOHN C LAURIE

ONE OF THE BEST MEASURES OF A SUCCESSFUL OFFICIAL OR CREW IS HOW THEY RESPOND TO A MISTAKE MADE DURING THE GAME.

WE TEND NOT TO BELIEVE IN OURSELVES OR THE CREW UNTIL AFTER WE SURVIVE THE FIRST CRITICAL MISTAKE.

JOHN C LAURIE

THE CHANCES OF MAKING AN OFFICIATING MISTAKE INCREASE FIFTY PERCENT IF THE OFFICIAL IS SURPRISED BY THE PLAY.

A GOOD CREW DOES NOT LET THE
ROOKIE ADDED TO THE CREW FEEL LIKE
A SIDE DISH THEY DIDN'T ORDER.

JOHN C LAURIE

THE BEST REFEREES HAVE THE BEST
CREWS BECAUSE THEY HAVE FOUND
A WAY TO GIVE PRAISE LOUDLY AND
EXPRESS BLAME SLOWLY.

IN THE POST-GAME CONVERSATIOIN WITH THE CREW, CELEBRATE WHAT YOU WANT TO SEE MORE OF.

JOHN C LAURIE

THE GREATEST EVIDENCE OF A SUPERIOR EXPERIENCED OFFICIAL IS THAT DURING A GAME HE IS NOT REALLY SURPRISED BY ANYTHING

IF YOU HAVE TO ASK WHAT IT FEELS LIKE TO WORK A NEAR-PERFECT GAME, YOU WILL NEVER KNOW.

JOHN C LAURIE

IT IS A GOOD PLAN WHEN STARTING OUT IN OFFICIATING TO HAVE SOME REALISTIC KNOWLEDGE ABOUT HOW LONG IT WILL TAKE YOU TO SUCCEED.

A CREW MEMBER THAT HAS HAD A GAME
OF HARD KNOCKS CAN USE A FEW SOFT
TOUCHES FROM THE CREW.

JOHN C LAURIE

THE BEST OFFICIATING CREWS DO THEIR
BASIC RESPONSIBILITIES VERY WELL
AND THE DIFFICULT THINGS BETTER
THAN MOST.

DURING MOST OF WHAT HAPPENS IN A FOOTBALL GAME, THE MOST IMPORTANT PARTS ARE THE MOST SIMPLE.

JOHN C LAURIE

THE BEST OFFICIALS USE THEIR SUPERIOR JUDGEMENT TO AVOID SITUATIONS WHICH REQUIRE THE USE OF THEIR SUPERIOR SKILL!

YOUR OFFICIATING SUCCESS MAY
DEPEND LESS ON ADVICE YOU ACCEPT
THAN ON ADVICE YOU IGNORE.

JOHN C LAURIE

WHEN YOU THROW YOUR FLAG, YOU
ARE EITHER PART OF THE PROBLEM OR
PART OF THE SOLUTION. DON'T STOP
OFFICIATING AT THIS POINT.

THE BEST REFEREES, WHEN DEALING
WITH THEIR CREW OR A COACH, ARE
GOOD LISTENERS.

JOHN C LAURIE

ONCE YOU HAVE TRAVELLED DOWN
THE ROAD OF SOME DIFFICULT GAMES
SUCCESSFULLY, THE ROAD IS NEVER
AS LONG.

AS A REFEREE, WORK TO DEVELOP THE CONFIDENCE OF YOUR CREW AS OPPOSED TO THEIR AFFECTION.

JOHN C LAURIE

SOME OFFICIALS ARE LUCKY AND SOME HAVE SKILL. THE BEST WAY TO TELL ONE QUALITY FROM THE OTHER IS TIME!

THE BEST OFFICIALS HAVE THE ABILITY AFTER MAKING A MISTAKE TO REMAIN FOCUSED AND KEEP THEIR ENTHUSIASM.

JOHN C LAURIE

THE BEST DEFINITION OF HAVING A GOOD FIRST GAME AS AN OFFICIAL IS SIMPLY THE TRIUMPH OF HOPE OVER EXPERIENCE.

THE MARK OF AN EFFECTIVE REFEREE
AS A CREW LEADER IS THAT HE ALWAYS
GIVES MORE THAN HE GETS.

JOHN C LAURIE

ONE OF THE GREATEST PLEASURES OF A
BEGINNING OR EXPERIENCED OFFICIAL
IS DOING WHAT OTHER PEOPLE SAID YOU
COULDN'T DO.

WELL-PLACED MISTAKES IN A GAME, WITH A LITTLE LUCK AND PREVIOUS PREPARATION, CAN TURN INTO SUCCESS.

JOHN C LAURIE

WISE, EXPERIENCED OFFICIALS REALIZE THAT EVEN DOING WHAT IS RIGHT IS NO GUARANTEE AGAINST MISFORTUNE.

EVERY REFEREE SHOULD HAVE A FAIR-SIZED CEMETERY IN WHICH TO BURY THE FAULTS OF HIS CREW.

JOHN C LAURIE

REALITY IS WHAT DOESN'T GO AWAY WHEN YOU STOP BELIEVING THAT YOU WERE A LOT BETTER THAN YOU REALLY WERE.

SOMETIMES THE SECRET OF WORKING A GREAT GAME DEPENDS ON WHAT YOU DON'T DO.

JOHN C LAURIE

IT TAKES A LOT OF RESTRAINT FOR AN OFFICIAL DURING AN INTENSE GAME TO LEARN AND PRACTICE THE IMPORTANCE OF PATIENCE.

GOOD CREWS MAKE GOOD THINGS HAPPEN IN A GOOD OR DIFFICULT GAME TO OFFICIATE.

JOHN C LAURIE

IT IS EASIER FOR AN OLDER OFFICIAL TO SHOW VIGOR AND ENERGY THAN IT IS FOR A YOUNG OFFICIAL TO SHOW WISDOM.

THE MOST SUCCESSFUL CREWS FIND A WAY TO PREPARE FOR LUCK JUST IN CASE IT HAPPENS.

JOHN C LAURIE

HOW YOU WEAR YOUR UNIFORM IS VERY IMPORTANT, BUT YOUR EXPRESSIONS AND GESTURES CAN DO MORE HARM THAN GOOD.

WHEN IT IS NOT NECESSARY TO CALL A FOUL, IT IS NECESSARY NOT TO CALL A FOUL.

JOHN C LAURIE

FORMULA TO BE A GOOD OFFICIAL:
25% KNOWLEDGE
25% EXPERIENCE
50% COMMON SENSE

THE ALL AMERICAN CREW

Not sure there has ever been a college crew with more NFL history than this one – Big 8 Missouri crew 1989.

L-R: Butch Clark, Terry Turlington, J. C. Leimbach (NFL), Bruce Finlayson, Supervisor (NFL), Mark Hittner (NFL), George Hayward (NFL), Mike Weir (NFL), Mike Borgard (NFL)

WHEN A COACH SWEARS (PERSONAL) AT YOU, PENALIZE, AVOID A PERSONAL RESPONSE OR GESTURES AND MOVE ON!

JOHN C LAURIE

YOU HAVE WON YOUR CREW AS THEIR REFEREE WHEN THEY WILL SHARE THEIR GOALS, PROBLEMS AND REWARDS WITH YOU.

THE BEST CREWS HAVE THE ABILITY TO HAVE EVERY COACH IN THE LEAGUE FEEL HE IS THE BEST.

JOHN C LAURIE

WHEN EXPERIENCED OFFICIALS DON'T HELP OTHERS, BOTH LOSE; THOSE THAT SHARE THEIR SKILL IN THE END ARE WINNERS.

VERY SELDOM IS IT EVER TOO LATE TO
BECOME WHAT YOU HAD THE POTENTIAL
TO BE IN OFFICIATING.

JOHN C LAURIE

A GOOD REFEREE, LIKE A GOOD
SHEPHERD, SHEARS HIS FLOCK ONCE
IN A WHILE BUT TRIES NOT TO SKIN
MEMBERS OF HIS CREW.

SOME GAMES REQUIRE THAT YOU SWIM THROUGH THE CRAP. THE SECRET IS NOT TO "BOB" IN IT.

JOHN C LAURIE

FINDING ONE THING IN THE GAME TO IMPROVE ON NEXT WEEK IS THE BEST WAY TO PUSH YOURSELF TO MAKE PROGRESS.

A GOOD OFFICIAL WILL SOLVE
PROBLEMS ON THE FIELD;
THE BEST OFFICIALS FIND WAYS TO
AVOID HAVING PROBLEMS.

JOHN C LAURIE

KNOW SOME PART OF THE GAME BETTER
THAN ANY OTHER MEMBER OF THE
CREW, SHARE IT, AND YOUR CREW WILL
BECOME BETTER EACH WEEK.

A GOOD TECHNIQUE FOR AN OFFICIAL IS
TO KNOW WHEN TO LET A CONFLICT DIE.

JOHN C LAURIE

ERROR IS A HARDY PLANT WITHIN THE
GRASS OF EVERY FOOTBALL FIELD.
WITHIN YOUR CREW, PULL THE WEEDS
AND DON'T OVER-FERTILIZE.

GOOD CREWS NOT ONLY TAKE
RESPONSIBILITY AND CREDIT FOR
GAMES THAT GO WELL BUT ALSO THAT
GO POORLY.

JOHN C LAURIE

A GOOD REFEREE WILL SEE SOME
GOOD IN EVERY MEMBER OF HIS CREW
EVEN IF HE NEEDS TO SQUINT FROM
TIME TO TIME.

IF YOU ARE GOING TO PROFIT FROM YOUR MISTAKES, YOU ARE GOING TO MAKE SOME.

JOHN C LAURIE

THERE IS THE APPEARANCE OF ONLY A SLIGHT DIFFERENCE BETWEEN PATIENCE AND LAZINESS. GOOD OFFICIALS KNOW THE DIFFERENCE.

WHEN THINGS ARE CONFUSING, AN
OUNCE OF PATIENCE IS WORTH A POUND
OF BRAINS.

JOHN C LAURIE

"BUMPS" IN A GAME MEAN THAT
YOU ARE EITHER HEADED FOR A RUT OR
COMING OUT OF ONE. THE CHOICE
IS YOURS.

OFFICIATING IS A BALANCE BETWEEN PREVENTABLE ACTS AND APPROPRIATE REACTION.

JOHN C LAURIE

THE ALPHABET OF A SUCCESSFUL OFFICIATING CAREER BEGINS WITH:
ABILITY,
BREAKS,
COURAGE.

HAVING THE RIGHT PHILOSOPHY
REGARDING THE GAME OF FOOTBALL
CREATES A "FLOW OF COMMON SENSE.

JOHN C LAURIE

SUCCESS IS THE PROGRESSIVE
REALIZATION OF THE WORTHY GOAL OF
IMPROVING EACH GAME YOU OFFICIATE.

THE PREVENTION OF PROBLEMS DURING THE GAME IS BETTER THAN ANY CURE YOU CAN THINK OF.

JOHN C LAURIE

THE BEST CREW WILL ALWAYS FIND A TIMELY WAY TO ADJUST TO THE CHANGING OF CONDITIONS DURING THE GAME.

CONSISTENT COMMON SENSE WILL
EXTEND YOUR CAREER LONGER THAN
ANY OTHER SINGLE QUALITY.

JOHN C LAURIE

ACCEPTING THE RESULT OF A MISTAKE IS
THE FIRST AND MOST IMPORTANT STEP
IN THE PREVENTION OF ANOTHER ONE
JUST ABOUT TO OCCUR.

IT IS OKAY TO BE ON TOP OF THE HEAP;
JUST REMEMBER THAT YOU ARE STILL
PART OF THE HEAP.

JOHN C LAURIE

KNOW THE DIFFERENCE BETWEEN
URGENT AND IMPORTANT SITUATIONS
THAT OCCUR DURING A FOOTBALL GAME.

IF YOU DON'T ENJOY OFFICIATING UNTIL YOU RETIRE, YOU MISSED HALF OF THE GAME.

> JOHN C LAURIE

OFFICIALS ARE DIVIDED INTO TWO CLASSES: THOSE WHO WANT TO BECOME SOMEONE AND THOSE WHO WANT TO ACCOMPLISH SOMETHING.

IT IS NOT AS IMPORTANT HOW MUCH YOU LEARN AS AN OFFICIAL AS HOW LITTLE YOU FORGET.

JOHN C LAURIE

THE QUALITY OF COMMON SENSE IN AN OFFICIAL IS THE CAPACITY TO SEE THINGS AS THEY ARE AND THEN DO WHAT NEEDS TO BE DONE.

THE BEST REFEREES FIND THE ABILITY TO BE A BRIDGE TO EACH OF THEIR CREW MEMBERS.

JOHN C LAURIE

IT IS OKAY TO HAVE AN ABNORMAL REACTION TO AN ABNORMAL SITUATION BUT COMMON SENSE WILL INSURE THE CORRECT CONCLUSION.

AN OFFICIAL CAN PROFIT FROM GOOD EXPERIENCES DURING A GAME AND LEARN FROM BAD ONES.

JOHN C LAURIE

THE REAL SUCCESS IN BECOMING A SUCCESSFUL OFFICIAL IS OVERCOMING THE FEAR OF BEING UNSUCCESSFUL.

THE RULE BOOK TEACHES OFFICIALS THE RULES AND EXPERIENCE TEACHES THEM THE EXCEPTIONS.

JOHN C LAURIE

THE NEXT BEST THING TO SOLVING A DIFFICULT PROBLEM DURING A STRESSFUL GAME IS TO FIND SOME HUMOR IN IT.

NEVER THINK YOU HAVE "SEEN IT ALL" IN OFFICIATING BECAUSE THAT IS WHEN _ _IT HAPPENS.

JOHN C LAURIE

YOUR BEST FRIEND IN THE CREW WILL STAB YOU IN THE CHEST. YOU CAN IMPROVE AND HEAL WITH THIS KIND OF WOUND.

WHEN THINGS GO WRONG POOR
OFFICIALS FIND PLENTY OF
EXCUSE. GOOD OFFICIALS USE ONE
REASON—"MYSELF."

JOHN C LAURIE

OFFICIALS GO THROUGH A REVOLVING
DOOR MANY TIMES IN THEIR CAREERS;
THE ONES WHO COME OUT AHEAD ARE
THE ONES WITH CONFIDENCE.

WHEN THERE IS CONFUSION ON THE FIELD, ACTION IS THE BEST REMEDY TO REGAIN CONTROL.

JOHN C LAURIE

THE BEST CREWS WORK HIGH PROFILE GAMES, RISE TO THE OCCASION, AND SLIP QUIETLY AWAY UNNOTICED WHEN IT IS OVER.

IF YOUR CONSCIENCE "HURTS" WHEN
EVERYONE ELSE THINKS YOU DID A
GREAT JOB, LEARN FROM EXPERIENCE.

JOHN C LAURIE

THE FIRST STEP IN OFFICIATING A GREAT
GAME IS A GOOD PREGAME;
THE ALTERNATIVE IS WORKING THE
GAME ON ONE LEG.

AN OUNCE OF PERFORMANCE ON THE FIELD IS WORTH A POUND OF DISCUSSION IN THE PREGAME.

JOHN C LAURIE

GOOD OFFICIALS LEARN FROM THEIR MISTAKES. THE BEST OFFICIALS LEARN FROM THEIR MISTAKES PLUS THE MISTAKES OF OTHERS.

THE BEST OFFICIALS GAIN CONFIDENCE FROM THE EXPERIENCE OF A MISTAKE; POOR OFFICIALS CRUMBLE.

JOHN C LAURIE

WHEN THE GAME LOSES ITS FLOW AND IS OUT OF SYNC, FIND A WAY TO ENJOY THE SCENERY AS YOU WORK THROUGH THE DETOUR.

IT IS BETTER TO BE MORE CONCERNED ABOUT A MEAN COACH THAN ONE WHO DOES NOT KNOW THE RULES.

JOHN C LAURIE

THE BEST OFFICIALS FIND THE NITCH OF BEING COMFORTABLE AT A LEVEL AT WHICH THEIR TALENT LEVEL IS NEAR THEIR EXPECTATIONS.

THE ABILITY TO ANTICIPATE AND PREPARE FOR THE UNEXPECTED IS THE SIGN OF A GOOD EXPERIENCED OFFICIAL.

JOHN C LAURIE

TOUGH GAMES REVEAL THE QUALITY AND CHARACTER OF AN OFFICIAL. GAMES EASY TO OFFICIATE CONCEAL A LOT OF THINGS.

GOOD MECHANICS ARE DEVELOPED FROM A HABIT THAT IS LONG ENOUGH CONTINUED.

JOHN C LAURIE

GOOD CREWS, LIKE BAD CREWS, HAVE MISSTEPS IN GAMES. THE DIFFERENCE IS THAT GOOD CREWS FIND A WAY TO STEP IN THE RIGHT DIRECTION.

OFFICIATING A FOOTBALL GAME IS A SERIES OF MAKING MULTIPLE DECISIONS EACH PLAY AND BETWEEN PLAYS.

JOHN C LAURIE

THE BEST CREWS ARE SIMPLIFIERS OF A COMPLICATED, EMOTIONAL AND SOMETIMES VIOLENT GAME.

IF YOU REALLY WANT TO LEARN FROM YOUR GAME FILM, TRY TRACING THE EFFECTS TO WHAT CAUSED THE PROBLEM.

JOHN C LAURIE

WHEN YOU ADVANCE FROM THE YOUNGEST IN THE CREW OR CONFERENCE TO THE OLDEST, TRY TO BE THE "YOUTH OF OLD AGE."

YOUR BEHAVIOR ON THE FIELD DURING A
DIFFICULT MOMENT SHOWS YOUR TRUE
IMAGE AS AN OFFICIAL.

JOHN C LAURIE

FOOTBALL OFFICIATING IS A WONDERFUL
AVOCATION. IF YOU REALIZE THIS
DURING YOUR CAREER, YOU WILL ENJOY
IT MORE LATER.

WHEN ANGRY WITH A COACH,
REMEMBER THAT SOONER OR LATER
MUDDY WATER CLEARS UP IF YOU LEAVE
IT ALONE.

JOHN C LAURIE

A GOOD REFEREE WILL CONVINCE HIS
CREW THAT SELF-INTEREST IS NOT AS
IMPORTANT AS CREW INTEREST.

YOU DON'T HAVE TO BE KIND TO BE AN OFFICIAL, BUT YOU HAVE TO BE KIND TO BE A GOOD ONE.

JOHN C LAURIE

NOT HELPING MEMBERS OF YOUR OWN CREW TO IMPROVE IS LIKE BURNING DOWN YOUR HOME TO GET RID OF A RAT.

THE BEST OFFICIALS LEARN SOMETHING BEYOND WHAT THEY HAVE ALREADY MASTERED IN EACH GAME.

JOHN C LAURIE

DOING NOTHING INSTEAD OF SOMETHING IN A GAME CRISIS SITUATION IS USUALLY THE QUICKEST WAY TO MAKE SOMETHING WORSE.

OFFICIATING INTELLIGENCE IS
ACCURATELY SEEING THINGS AS
THEY ARE, NOT WHAT COACHES AND
FANS SEE.

JOHN C LAURIE

IN A HEATED CREW DISCUSSION
OVER A CONTROVERSIAL ISSUE, DON'T
ALLOW THE CREW TO FIND FAULT;
FIND A REMEDY.

GOOD OFFICIALS REALIZE THAT SIMPLY DOING THE RIGHT THING DOES NOT MAKE YOU A POPULAR OFFICIAL.

JOHN C LAURIE

WHEN BEING PROACTIVE AND PREVENTIVE IN OFFICIATING, WEAR GLOVES. WHEN IT COMES TIME TO TAKE CONTROL OF THE GAME, BE BAREFISTED.

IT ISN'T YOUR POSITION ON THE CREW
THAT MAKES YOU SUCCESSFUL; IT'S
YOUR DISPOSITION.

JOHN C LAURIE

IN A TOUGH SITUATION THOUGHT AND
THEORY ARE IMPORTANT, BUT YOU
REACH A POINT WHERE TAKING ACTION
PREVAILS.

ONE OF THE BEST MEASURES OF A GOOD CREW IS HOW LONG IT TAKES THEM TO FIND OUT THEY WERE WRONG.

JOHN C LAURIE

AN OFFICIAL WITH AVERAGE SKILLS AND HIGH CONFIDENCE WILL OUT-PERFORM ONE WITH HIGH SKILLS AND LOW SELF-CONFIDENCE.

WHEN TWO OFFICIALS THROW A FLAG
ON A PLAY, THE QUESTION IS NOT WHO IS
RIGHT BUT WHAT IS RIGHT.

JOHN C LAURIE

HINDSIGHT AND FORESIGHT ARE
GOOD IN BUSINESS BUT GOOD EYESIGHT
IS REQUIRED TO BE A GOOD FOOTBALL
OFFICIAL.

THE BEST OFFICIALS HAVE THE TALENT OF BEING ABLE TO DISAGREE WITH A COACH AND NOT BE DISAGREEABLE.

JOHN C LAURIE

THE BEST OFFICIAL DOES NOT PERMIT UNNECESSARY THOUGHTS TO GO BEYOND THE SITUATION WITH WHICH HE IS DEALING.

THE BEST REFEREES, AFTER THE CREW HAS OFFICIATED A GREAT GAME, REMEMBER TO PASS THE PRIDE DOWN.

JOHN C LAURIE

THE REASON THAT THINGS TURN OUT BEST ON THE BEST CREWS IS THAT THEY FIND A WAY TO MAKE THE BEST OF EACH SITUATION.

A GOOD MECHANIC TO DEVELOP
IN OFFICIATING IS TO PRACTICE
CORRECTING YOUR BAD HABITS.

JOHN C LAURIE

OFFICIALS IMPROVE BY GETTING IT
RIGHT THE FIRST TIME AND, WHEN IT IS
DONE WRONG, GETTING IT RIGHT THE
SECOND TIME.

THE DIFFERENCE BETWEEN OFFICIATING A GOOD GAME AND A GREAT GAME IS HOW THE CREW HANDLES PLAN B.

JOHN C LAURIE

GOOD OFFICIALS ANTICIPATE THE PLAY; THE BEST OFFICIALS ANTICIPATE THE CONSEQUENCES OF A PLAY THAT MAY COME TO THEM.

MATURE OFFICIALS AND CREWS HAVE THE ABILITY AND CAPACITY TO ENDURE UNCERTAINTY.

JOHN C LAURIE

IF YOU TAKE THE TIME TO SET A GOOD EXAMPLE FOR THE "ROOKIE" ON YOUR CREW, YOU ARE REALLY IMPROVING TWO OFFICIALS.

A GOOD GOAL FOR AN OFFICIATING CREW IS NOT TO BE PERFECT BUT TO PROGRESS EACH WEEK.

JOHN C LAURIE

THE BEST OFFICIALS HAVE THE ABILITY TO LOOK BACK ON THEIR CAREER WITH GRATITUDE AND TO THE NEXT GAME WITH CONFIDENCE.

THE SECRET OF AN EFFECTIVE CAREER LIES IN THE CREW'S ABILITY TO ORGANIZE THE NON-OBVIOUS.

JOHN C LAURIE

IT IS WISE TO REMEMBER THAT EVEN AN OFFICIAL IN PERFECT POSITION ON THE FIELD CAN STILL BE WRONG DURING THE GAME.

IT IS OKAY TO BE WRONG IF IT MAKES
YOU A WISER AND BETTER OFFICIAL
THAN YOU WERE YOUR LAST GAME.

JOHN C LAURIE

IT IS IMPORTANT TO KNOW WHAT TO DO
IN OFFICIATING A GAME BUT IT IS EVEN
MORE IMPORTANT TO KNOW WHAT TO
DO NEXT.

THE BEST OFFICIALS KNOW HOW TO ACCEPT REJECTION AND ALSO TO REJECT ACCEPTANCE.

JOHN C LAURIE

YOU MUST HAVE THE CONFIDENCE YOU ARE SUPERIOR TO THE CIRCUMTANCE TO GET THROUGH THE TOUGH ONES.

THE BEST OFFICIALS NEVER FORGET WHAT IS WORTH REMEMBERING OR REMEMBER WHAT IS BEST FORGOTTEN.

JOHN C LAURIE

IF AN OFFICIAL HAS TWO ARMS AND ONLY ONE COMMON SENSE AND IS FACED WITH A CHOICE, IT IS BETTER TO LOSE AN ARM.

Dr. John Laurie

CELEBRATING MIKE LINER'S BIRTHDAY

Having fun at appropriate times is always important for a crew.

L-R: John Laurie, Brad Horschem, Tim Crowley, Phil Laurie, (middle) Mike Liner

SHOW ME A GOOD REFEREE AND I CAN IDENTIFY HIS CREW. SHOW ME A GOOD CREW AND I CAN IDENTIFY THEIR REFEREE.

JOHN C LAURIE

A GOOD REFEREE WILL SHOW TOLERANCE WHEN HE IS IN THE MAJORITY WITH HIS CREW AND COURAGE WHEN HE IS IN THE MINORITY.

A GOOD REPLAY OFFICIAL HAS
THE ABILITY TO TAKE AS LONG AS
NECESSARY TO MAKE A SNAP DECISION.

JOHN C LAURIE

TO A BOOK OFFICIAL THE GAME IS
THEORY. GOOD OFFICIALS GET BEYOND
THE RULE BOOK AND UNDERSTAND
WHAT IS GOING ON.

THE BEST CREWS FIND WAYS TO CREATE CIRCUMSTANCES THAT ALLOW THE GAME TO FLOW SMOOTHLY AND FAIRLY.

JOHN C LAURIE

THE QUALITY OF THE REFEREE'S EXPECTATION OF HIMSELF AND THE CREW DETERMINES THE QUALITY OF THE CREW.

YOUR DEGREE OF DETERMINATION DETERMINES YOUR DESTINY AS AN OFFICIAL.

JOHN C LAURIE

WHETHER YOU HAVE A VERY LONG OR A VERY SHORT CAREER, HUMILITY IS ALWAYS ONLY ONE "SNAP" AWAY.

FOR A ROOKIE OFFICIAL AND ONE
NEARING THE END OF HIS CAREER,
ENTHUSIASM IS HIS BEST PROTECTOR.

JOHN C LAURIE

A WELL-OFFICIATED FOOTBALL GAME IS
LIKE MOST CARD GAMES—SOME LUCK
PLUS A LOT OF SKILL AND PREPARATION.

WHEN YOU CAN'T BE PERFECT WITH A DIFFICULT SITUATION DURING THE GAME—BE FAIR!

JOHN C LAURIE

A FOOTBALL CREW THAT GENUINELY TRUSTS AND RESPECTS EACH OTHER WILL MAKE THE FEWEST MISTAKES.

IT IS NOT OKAY TO IGNORE A GUT
FEELING DURING THE GAME—JUST DON'T
BELIEVE IT IS ENOUGH.

JOHN C LAURIE

RATHER THAN ARGUE WITH A COACH
ABOUT THE WRONG ANSWER,
TRY TO AGREE ON THE CORRECT
QUESTION FIRST.

GOOD CREWS DO NOT HAVE AN ABSENCE OF CONFLICT; THEY SIMPLY FIND A WAY TO MANAGE IT.

JOHN C LAURIE

THINK GENERALITIES OF SITUATIONS IN THE PREGAME AND THEN FOCUS ON DETAILS DURING THE GAME.

WHETHER AN OFFICIAL IS IMPROVING OR REGRESSING, THERE IS BOTH INTERNAL AND EXTERNAL IMPETUS.

JOHN C LAURIE

GOOD OFFICIALS ACCEPT THE FACT THAT AT TIMES EVEN DOING WHAT IS RIGHT IN A GAME CAN STILL BRING MISFORTUNE.

YOU DON'T WIN EVERY PLAY, EVERY
QUARTER OR EVEN EVERY GAME.
SOMETIMES THE DRAGON WINS.

JOHN C LAURIE

THE REAL RESPONSIBILITY OF
THE REFEREE WITH AN EXPERIENCED
CREW IS NOT LETTING THEM GET OLD
ON THE JOB.

IF A CREW HAS TWO LEADERS EVERY TIME, THEY WILL FADE AND DISAPPEAR FOR LACK OF UNITY.

JOHN C LAURIE

DURING A BENCH-CLEARING FIGHT, KEEP YOUR MOTOR IDLING EVEN THOUGH YOU FEEL LIKE STRIPPING YOUR GEARS.

SOMETIMES DOING YOUR BEST WON'T GET THE JOB DONE; YOU MUST DO WHAT IS NECESSARY.

JOHN C LAURIE

A CREW OF LIONS LED BY A DONKEY WILL USUALLY RESULT IN A BUNCH OF "ASSES" OFFICIATING A GAME.

AN OFFICIAL IS JUDGED BY HIS PERFORMANCE ON THE FIELD AND NOT HIS WORDS DURING THE PREGAME.

JOHN C LAURIE

THE REFEREE (LEADER) WHO ENJOYS SHARING RESPONSIBILITY KEEPS IT AND THE REFEREE WHO EXERCISES HIS AUTHORITY LOSES IT.

THE MORE EFFECTIVE THE REFEREE IS WITH THE CREW, THE LESS DIRECT CONTROL HE NEEDS TO LEAD.

JOHN C LAURIE

IN ORDER TO KNOW WHICH STRINGS TO PULL WITH YOUR CREW AND COACHES, IT HELPS TO ALSO KNOW THE ROPES.

SILENCE IS THE BEST SUBSTITUTE FOR BRAINS WHEN TALKING TO AN ANGRY COACH.

JOHN C LAURIE

DON'T JUDGE AN OFFICIAL BY HIS OPINIONS IN THE PREGAME MEETING. JUDGE HIM BY WHAT HE DOES WITH HIS OPINIONS ON THE FIELD.

A CREW WITH MULTIPLE LEADERS WILL FADE AND BECOME INEFFECTIVE BY THE END OF THE SEASON.

JOHN C LAURIE

THE KEY TO OFFICIATING A GREAT GAME IS TO JOIN A GOOD START TO A GOOD ENDING WITH A SMOOTH "FLOW" IN THE MIDDLE.

SOMETIMES THE DIFFERENCE BETWEEN FACT AND FICTION IS HAVING THE ABILITY NOT TO BE A "BALL WATCHER."

JOHN C LAURIE

GREAT GAMES ARE OFFICIATED BY CREWS WITH GREAT PERSEVERANCE AND CONCENTRATION ON EACH PLAY.

KNOWLEDGE DOES NOT TAKE THE PLACE OF SIMPLE OBSERVATION. SEE THE PLAY; MAKE THE CALL!

JOHN C LAURIE

THE DIFFERENCE BETWEEN A SUCCESSFUL AND AN UNSUCCESSFUL OFFICIAL IS THE MANNER IN WHICH HE OVERCOMES HIS BLUNDERS.

THE KEY TO COMMUNICATING WITH
A DIFFICULT COACH IS TO USE SOFT
WORDS AND HARD ARGUMENTS.

JOHN C LAURIE

THE FIRST STEP TO BECOMING
A GOOD OFFICIAL IS UNDERSTANDING
WHAT YOU DON'T KNOW AND THEN
FINDING A WAY TO KNOW IT.

AN EFFECTIVE REFEREE DOES NOT "DISCIPLINE" HIS CREW BUT FINDS POSITIVE WAYS TO MOTIVATE THEM.

JOHN C LAURIE

IF YOU HAVE ESTABLISHED A POSITIVE RELATIONSHIP WITH A COACH, YOU CAN OFTEN PERSUADE HIM WHEN YOU CAN'T CONVINCE HIM.

THE TRUE COLORS OF THE RULE BOOK ARE NOT BLACK AND WHITE BUT SHADES OF GRAY.

JOHN C LAURIE

WHEN THE REFEREE IS TRYING TO IMPROVE A CREW MEMBER OR THE CREW, HE CANNOT ANTAGONIZE AND INFLUENCE AT THE SAME TIME.

THE ONLY DECISIVE QUALITY IN POOR OFFICIALS IS THEIR ABILITY TO AVOID MAKING DECISIONS.

JOHN C LAURIE

THE BEST REFEREES DEMONSTRATE AN INFLUENCE OVER THEIR CREWS WHILE SELDOM USING THEIR AUTHORITY.

A GOOD REFEREE AND BOXER SHARE
THE QUALITIES OF A GOOD PUNCH
(TALENT) AND CLEVER FOOTWORK (TACT).

JOHN C LAURIE

IT IS GOOD TO REMEMBER WHEN
CONFRONTED BY AN ANGRY COACH
THAT YOU CANNOT ANTAGONIZE AND
PERSUADE HIM AT THE SAME TIME.

THE BEST OFFICIALS ACT WHEN THE GAME BECOMES DIFFICULT; THE POOR OFFICIALS REACT.

JOHN C LAURIE

IT IS IMPORTANT THAT THE CREW BELIEVE IN THE REFEREE BUT IT IS MORE IMPORTANT THAT THE REFEREE BELIEVES IN THE CREW.

A CREW HAS A WAY OF BECOMING WHAT
THE REFEREE ENCOURAGES IT TO BE.

JOHN C LAURIE

ROOKIE OFFICIALS WOULD BE OFF TO A
BETTER START IF THEY REALIZED IT IS
BETTER TO PREVENT BAD HABITS THAN
TO BREAK THEM.

IT IS OKAY TO MAKE MISTAKES WHILE OFFICIATING A GAME—JUST DON'T MAKE THE "WRONG ONES."

JOHN C LAURIE

SUCCESSFUL OFFICIALS HAVE SIMPLY FORMED THE HABIT OF DOING THE THINGS THAT UNSUCCESSFUL OFFICIALS WILL NOT DO.

THE BEST REFEREES HAVE THE ABILITY TO CHANGE THEIR CREWS FROM WHAT THEY ARE TO WHAT THEY ARE TO BE.

JOHN C LAURIE

BEING THE REFEREE DOESN'T MEAN YOU ARE THE SMARTEST OFFICIAL ON THE CREW; IT JUST MEANS YOU ARE WEARING THE WHITE HAT.

THERE ARE TIMES IN AN OFFICIAL'S CAREER WHEN INTEGRITY MUST TAKE THE PLACE OVER CREW LOYALTY.

JOHN C LAURIE

THE BEST WAY TO DESCRIBE THE BEST REFEREES AND CREWS IS THAT THEY CONSISTENTLY TURN IN SUPERIOR PERFORMANCES.

OFFICIALS CLING TO HABITS AND SO DEVELOP THE HABIT OF GOOD OFFICIATING MECHANICS.

JOHN C LAURIE

THERE IS NOTHING LIKE A "CREATIVE" EXPERIENCE TO UPSET THE THEORY OF OFFICIATING FOR A BOOK OFFICIAL.

THE BEST WAY TO LEARN THE ROPES OF OFFICIATING IS BY UNTYING A FEW KNOTS ALONG THE WAY.

JOHN C LAURIE

THERE IS ONLY ONE THING IN OFFICIATING MORE CONTAGIOUS THAN MEASLES AND THAT IS THE REFEREE SETTING A GOOD EXAMPLE.

THE MOST IMPORTANT MAN ON THE CREW IS THE ONE WHO KNOWS WHAT THE RIGHT THING IS TO DO NEXT.

JOHN C LAURIE

THE BIGGEST MISTAKE THAT THE REFEREE CAN MAKE WHEN CONFRONTED BY AN IRATE COACH IS TO ANSWER THE QUESTION HE IS NOT ASKING.

SOME HEAD COACHES EXPECT "HOME" GAMES TO PROVIDE THEM WITH A "FAIR" ADVANTAGE.

JOHN C LAURIE

THE REFEREE MUST BE CLOSE ENOUGH TO HIS CREW TO RELATE TO THEM BUT FAR ENOUGH TO INDIVIDUALLY AND COLLECTIVELY MOTIVATE THEM.

WHY DO SOME PREGAME HANDSHAKES WITH THE HEAD COACH FEEL LIKE A TOURNIQUET?

JOHN C LAURIE

ONE OF THE BURDENS OF BEING AN EFFECTIVE REFEREE IS THAT THERE ARE TIMES WHEN YOU MUST BE UNPOPULAR.

THE VALUE OF A RULEBOOK IS NOT TO KNOW THE RULES BUT TO KNOW HOW TO APPLY THE RULES.

JOHN C LAURIE

WHEN ONE REFLECTS BACK ON HIS CAREER, IT WON'T BE THE GAMES, TEAMS OR SCORES; IT WILL BE THE MOMENTS THAT CREATED MEMORIES.

A SENSE OF HUMOR IS THE ONLY DART THAT AN OFFICIAL CAN USE TO STAB HIMSELF IN THE BACK.

JOHN C LAURIE

THE MOST CONTENTMENT AN OFFICIAL CAN HAVE IS TO BELIEVE THAT HE GAVE EVERYTHING HE HAD EVERY PLAY OF THE GAME.

THE ART OF BEING AN EFFECTIVE OFFICIAL IS ACTING RATIONAL WHEN DEALING WITH IRRATIONAL COACHES.

JOHN C LAURIE

BEWARE OF THE OFFICIAL WHO SEEMS TO MOVE AT TWICE THE SPEED OF SOUND AND HALF THE SPEED OF COMMON SENSE.

WHEN AN OFFICIAL NO LONGER CARES
WHAT OTHERS THINK ABOUT HIM, HE IS
EITHER AT THE TOP OR THE BOTTOM.

JOHN C LAURIE

SOME OF THE STRONGEST OFFICIALS
IN YOUR CONFERENCE HAVE USED THE
BRICKS THROWN AT THEM TO BUILD A
STRONG FOUNDATION FOR
THEIR SUCCESS.

THE DIFFERENCE BETWEEN GOOD AND BAD OFFICIATING SIMPLY BOILS DOWN TO CHOICES MADE ON THE FIELD.

JOHN C LAURIE

SOMETIMES ALL WE HAVE IS A GOOD HUNCH ON WHAT HAS HAPPENED. USUALLY A HUNCH IS BASED ON FACTS KEPT JUST BELOW YOUR LEVEL OF CONSCIOUSNESS.

IF AN OFFICIAL TAKES CARE OF HIS CHARACTER ON AND OFF THE FIELD, HIS REPUTATION WILL TAKE CARE OF ITSELF.

JOHN C LAURIE

AFTER A POORLY OFFICIATED GAME, IF YOU ARE DISSATISFIED WITHOUT BEING DISCOURAGED, YOU WILL MAKE APPROPRIATE PROGRESS WITH YOUR CAREER.

NEVER FEAR CRITICISM WHEN YOU ARE
RIGHT AND NEVER IGNORE CRITICISM
WHEN YOU ARE WRONG.

JOHN C LAURIE

IF YOUR CIRCLE OF KNOWLEDGE AND
YOUR CIRCLE OF EXPERIENCE ARE NOT
THE SAME, CONTINUE TO MAKE BOTH
LARGER AND CLOSER TO THE SAME SIZE.

THE BEST REFEREES ARE NOT ONLY SELF-CONFIDENT BUT HAVE CONFIDENCE IN THEIR CREWS.

JOHN C LAURIE

IT IS REALLY NOT WHERE YOU ARE IN YOUR OFFICIATING CAREER, BUT MORE IMPORTANTLY WHERE YOU SEEK TO BE THAT ALLOWS YOU TO IMPROVE.

A WHITE HAT (REFEREE) DOES NOT MAKE YOU A LEADER BUT GIVES YOU THE OPPORTUNITY TO BE ONE.

JOHN C LAURIE

WHATEVER YOUR GOAL IS IN OFFICIATING, YOU MUST SACRIFICE SOME CHOICES. THE KEY WILL BE TO KEEP YOUR SACRIFICES BALANCED APPROPRIATELY

THE BEST COACHES AND OFFICIALS AGREE TO DISAGREE EVEN WHEN THEY DON'T SEE EYE-TO-EYE.

JOHN C LAURIE

AS SOON AS YOU LEARN THAT SOME PROBLEMS DURING THE GAME SIMPLY NEED TO BE LIVED WITH, YOUR OFFICIATING EXPERIENCE WILL HAVE A BETTER FLOW TO IT.

THE REFEREE WHO LOVES A CREW THAT DOES NOT WANT TO WORK TOGETHER NEEDS TO BE PATIENTLY AGGRESSIVE.

JOHN C LAURIE

THE OFFICIAL WHO HAS AN EXCELLENT CAREER WAS PROBABLY AT THE RIGHT PLACE AT THE RIGHT TIME.
HE ALSO STEERED HIMSELF IN THE RIGHT DIRECTION.

AN OFFICIAL WHO CAN MASTER CONCENTRATION IS ON HIS WAY TO MASTERING OFFICIATING.

JOHN C LAURIE

THE QUESTION FOR A BEGINNING OFFICIAL WHO WORKS TO GET TO THE TOP IN OFFICIATING IS NOT "WHO IS GOING TO LET ME GET THERE?" BUT "WHO CAN STOP ME?"

IF IS DIFFICULT TO SURPRISE A CREW
THAT HAS BEEN PROPERLY PREPARED
IN PREGAME.

JOHN C LAURIE

WHEN A CREW COMES TOGETHER
AFTER A MISTAKE HAS BEEN MADE,
THERE ARE TWO OPTIONS FOR EACH
CREW MEMBER: FIND FAULT OR FIND
A REMEDY.

THE REFEREE WHO DEVELOPS HIS CREW ADDS; THE REFEREE WHO DEVELOPS OTHER REFEREES MULTIPLIES.

JOHN C LAURIE

IT IS OKAY FOR OFFICIALS TO HAVE FEAR. THE KEY IS TO BE STRONG ENOUGH TO KNOW THERE ARE MORE THINGS TO DEAL WITH DURING THE CRITICAL PARTS OF THE GAME.

THE BEST IMPACT A RETIRING REFEREE
CAN HAVE ON HIS CREW IS WHEN HIS
FOLLOWERS SUCCEED.

JOHN C LAURIE

BE PATIENT WITH YOUR OFFICIATING
CAREER. JUST BECAUSE YOU ARE NOT
SURE WHERE YOU ARE GOING DOESN'T
MEAN YOU ARE ON THE WRONG ROAD.

THE SINGLE MOST IMPORTANT FACTOR IN DETERMINING THE MORALE OF THE CREW IS THE REFEREE.

JOHN C LAURIE

IT IS NEVER TOO LATE TO BE AS GOOD AS YOU ARE BEFORE YOU MAKE A MISTAKE. IT IS NEVER TOO LATE TO BE AS GOOD AS YOU WERE AFTER YOU MAKE A MISTAKE.

FIRST DOWN

"If I just had RED CASHION'S voice!"

John Laurie

THE GOOD THING ABOUT A FEW HARD
BUMPS IN A GAME IS THAT IT USUALLY
MEANS YOU ARE GETTING OUT OF A RUT.

JOHN C LAURIE

AS A REFEREE, LEARNING TO SAY "NO"
AND REFUSING "FAVORS" ARE VALUABLE
TOOLS IN BECOMING A LEADER AND
MAINTAINING LEADERSHIP AT YOUR
POSITION.

MOST OFFICIALS ONLY ALLOW THEMSELVES TO BE AS SUCCESSFUL AS THEY DESERVE TO BE.

JOHN C LAURIE

IT IS EASY FOR POOR OFFICIATING TO RUIN A WELL-PLAYED GAME, AND RATHER DIFFICULT FOR A STRONG OFFICIATING CREW TO RUIN EVEN A POORLY PLAYED GAME.

THE SIMPLEST SOLUTION TO A COMPLEX
PROBLEM MAY NOT BE CORRECT, BUT IT
IS THE PLACE TO START.

JOHN C LAURIE

WHEN THE REFEREE OR ANOTHER CREW
MEMBER IS QUICKLY CLIMBING THE
LADDER OF SUCCESS, IT IS GOOD FOR
HIM TO REMEMBER THAT THE ENTIRE
CREW IS HOLDING THE LADDER.

IT IS NOT A FATAL FLAW TO BE A BOOK
OFFICIAL IF YOU GO ON TO LEARN THE
"GAME OF FOOTBALL."

JOHN C LAURIE

IF I COULD ASK A SINGLE QUESTION TO
SELECT ONE OF TWO OFFICIALS, I WOULD
ASK HOW HE RESPONDED WHEN HE
WAS UNDER FIRE AND A GREAT DEAL OF
PRESSIRE.

A REFEREE HAS NOT REALLY DEVELOPED
A SUCCESSFUL CREW UNTIL HE HAS
ALSO DEVELOPED A SUCCESSOR.

JOHN C LAURIE

THE BEST OFFICIALS ARE AT THEIR
BEST WITH DIFFICULT, CHALLENGING
GAMES WHILE POOR OFFICIALS ONLY
SHINE WITH GAMES THAT ARE EASY TO
OFFICIATE.

THE BEST OFFICIALS HAVE GIVEN A LOT
OF PRIOR THOUGHT WHEN REQUIRED TO
MAKE SUDDEN DECISIONS.

JOHN C LAURIE

A REFEREE GAINS THE RESPECT OF HIS
CREW BY SHOWING HIS INTEREST IN THE
CREW. A POOR REFEREE TRIES TO GET
THE CREW INTERESTED IN HIMSELF.

YOUR CONDUCT ON THE FIELD IS MORE IMPORTANT THAN WHAT YOU SAID IN THE PREGAME.

JOHN C LAURIE

GOALS ARE IMPORTANT ROAD SIGNS IN BECOMING GOOD OFFICIALS, BUT THE BEST OFFICIALS HAVE TURNED A FEW DETOURS INTO A MAJOR HIGHWAY OF SUCCESS.

THE REVIEW OF A BIG MISTAKE MADE IN OFFICIATING ALMOST ALWAYS BEGINS WITH A VERY SMALL MISCUE.

JOHN C LAURIE

THE CHOICES FROM JUDGMENT PLAYS ON THE FIELD WILL DETERMINE THE SUCCESS OF THE OFFICIAL MUCH MORE THAN A RULES TEST.

THE QUALITY OF THE REFEREE IS REFLECTED IN THE STANDARDS HE SETS FOR HIMSELF.

JOHN C LAURIE

TO BE UPSET THAT YOU ARE WORKING A HIGH SCHOOL GAME AND NOT A COLLEGE GAME ON SATURDAY IS A WASTE OF ENJOYING A GOOD FRIDAY NIGHT HIGH SCHOOL GAME.

THE OPPORTUNITY FOR YOU TO SUCCEED
AS AN OFFICIAL IS ALWAYS RIGHT
WHERE YOU ARE.

JOHN C LAURIE

THE BEST ADVICE I CAN GIVE A ROOKIE
OFFICIAL IS TO ACCEPT CRITICISM
AND GUIDANCE FROM AN EXCELLENT
OFFICIAL AND THEN WORK HIS TAIL OFF.

THE BEST CREWS HIDE THE AWKWARD PARTS OF THE GAME AND REMAIN UNNOTICED WHENEVER POSSIBLE.

JOHN C LAURIE

WHEN A DIFFICULT SITUATION ON THE FIELD CANNOT BE ALTERED, DON'T WASTE TIME OR ENERGY BEING DISSATISFIED; REMAIN FOCUSED AND MOVE ON.

THREE WORDS THAT CAN SOMETIMES IMPROVE YOUR RELATIONSHIP WITH A COACH:
"I DON'T KNOW."

JOHN C LAURIE

WHEN A RULE HAS NOT BEEN VIOLATED AND SOMETHING COULD BE DONE, THE BEST USE OF DISCRETION IS HAVING THE TACT TO NOT SEE WHAT COULDN'T BE HELPED.

SOMETIMES OFFICIALS GET BREAKS.
THE GOOD ONES KNOW HOW TO
SUCCESSFULLY USE THEM.

JOHN C LAURIE

IF YOU FORGET TO MENTION SOMETHING
DURING THE GAME THAT BEARS
REVEALING TO THE SUPERVISOR AFTER
THE GAME, YOU WILL BE IN TROUBLE
WITH YOUR CREW.

GOOD OFFICIALS DON'T NEED TO SEE
THROUGH SITUATIONS ON THE FIELD;
THEY NEED TO SEE INTO THEM.

JOHN C LAURIE

MOST FOOTBALL GAMES HAVE AT LEAST
ONE CRITICAL MOMENT; THE BEST
CREWS RECOGNIZE THESE SITUATIONS
AND HANDLE THEM APPROPRIATELY.

THE BEST WAY TO HANDLE A COACH WHO
TALKS WITHOUT LISTENING IS TO LISTEN
WITHOUT TALKING.

JOHN C LAURIE

KEEP THE BIG THINGS IN FOCUS DURING
THE GAME AND CONCENTRATE ON THE
SMALL THINGS EACH PLAY AND YOU
WILL HAVE OFFICIATED A GREAT GAME.

IN THE PRESENCE OF TROUBLE, SOME CREWS GROW WINGS WHILE OTHERS PURCHASE CRUTCHES.

JOHN C LAURIE

AN OFFICIAL WHO CANNOT SEE SEVERAL POSSIBILITIES OF PLAY SITUATIONS BEFORE THE SNAP IS A SLAVE TO HIS FIRST IMPRESSION OR INSTINCT OF THE PLAY.

IF COACHES SPEAK NEGATIVELY ABOUT YOU, OFFICIATE ON THE FIELD SO NO ONE WILL BELIEVE THEM.

JOHN C LAURIE

IF YOU WANT A SPARRING PARTNER TO CHECK YOUR CHARACTER AND CONFIDENCE IN A DIFFICULT GAME, CHECK YOUR READING ON THE ADVERSITY METER.

WHEN VISITING WITH A COACH, BEING AT A LOSS FOR WORDS HAS SAVED MANY AN OFFICIATING CAREER.

JOHN C LAURIE

WHEN YOU HAVE CORRECTED A MISTAKE MADE BY ANOTHER OFFICIAL AND JUST THE TWO OF YOU KNOW, IT IS THE HIGHEST LEVEL OF BEING A CREW MEMBER.

BEWARE OF THE COACH WHO WILL ONLY CORRECTLY QUOTE YOU IF IT IS SOMETHING THAT YOU WISH YOU HADN'T SAID.

JOHN C LAURIE

YOU WILL HAVE A MORE SATISFYING CAREER IF YOU HAVE ABILITY AND NO OPPORTUNITY THAN IF YOU HAVE THE OPPORTUNITY AND NO ABILITY.

EVEN IN OFFICIATING, DOING THE RIGHT THING IS NOT ALWAYS THE RIGHT THING TO DO.

JOHN C LAURIE

A GOOD PHILOSOPHY FOR ALL OFFICIALS IS TO REALIZE THAT SPORTS AND OFFICIATING ARE NOT A SCIENCE. IT IS BETTER TO BE GENERALLY CORRECT THAN PRECISELY WRONG.

IF IT IS POSSIBLE TO GO WITHOUT SAYING SOMETHING TO A COACH, DO NOT INSIST ON REPEATING IT.

JOHN C LAURIE

YOU CAN TELL A GOOD CREW FROM A POOR CREW AS THE GOOD ONES SIMPLIFY COMPLEXITIES WHILE POOR CREWS COMPLICATE SIMPLE SITUATIONS ON THE FIELD.

SOME EXPERIENCE AND A HANDFUL OF COMMON SENSE ARE WORTH A BUSHEL OF RULE BOOKS.

JOHN C LAURIE

BE ALERT FOR CRITICAL AND DIFFICULT SITUATIONS THAT ARISE DURING A GAME. IT IS A GREAT CHANCE FOR YOUR CREW TO SHOW THEIR SKILLS, CONFIDENCE AND ABILITY.

IF THE REFEREE CAN'T DISCIPLINE
HIMSELF, HE CAN'T DISCIPLINE OR
LEAD OTHERS.

JOHN C LAURIE

THE PILL I WOULD LIKE TO GIVE EVERY
OFFICIAL IS TO KNOW AT THE TIME THAT
WHAT YOU ARE EXPERIENCING AS AN
OFFICIAL IS SO VERY SPECIAL.

THE BEST REFEREE DOESN'T TRY TO SEE THROUGH HIS CREW; HE TRIES TO SEE THEM THROUGH.

JOHN C LAURIE

A GOOD FOOTBALL GAME FLOWS LIKE READING A GOOD BOOK. HALF OF WHAT HAPPENS IS THE RULE BOOK; THE REST COMES FROM WISDOM AND GOOD JUDGMENT.

THERE IS NO LIMIT TO HOW HIGH AN OFFICIAL CAN GO IN OFFICIATING IF HE IS ON THE LEVEL.

JOHN C LAURIE

COMPORTMENT IS AN OFFICIAL'S ABILITY TO ACHIEVE SILENT ACCEPTANCE BY HIS ACTIONS AS AN OFFICIAL WHEN THERE IS HIGH ANXIETY ON THE FIELD.

THE BEST COMMUNICATORS ON THE CREW KNOW THAT NOT EVERY QUESTION A COACH ASKS REQUIRES AN ANSWER.

JOHN C LAURIE

LOOK THE PART. THE APPEARANCE OF SUCCESS CAN COVER A LOT OF GRAY AREAS BETWEEN THE CLEAR BLACK OR WHITE CALLS IN A FOOTBALL GAME.

THE BEST OFFICIALS DON'T TELL A COACH WHAT THEY THINK; THEY TELL HIM WHAT THEY KNOW.

JOHN C LAURIE

IT TAKES A BOW AND ARROWS TO OFFICIATE A GOOD GAME. RULES THAT ARE UNDERSTOOD ARE GREAT ARROWS, BUT IT IS THE BOW OF JUDGMENT THAT COMPLETES THE TASK.

IT IS SOMETIMES BETTER TO LEAVE A
COACH WONDERING WHY YOU DIDN'T
RESPOND THAN WHY YOU DID.

JOHN C LAURIE

WHEN MY BROTHER WHOSE BASEMENT
IS A FOOTBALL SHRINE WENT TO A
TROPHY SHOP, HIS COMMENT WAS, "BOY
THIS GUY IS REALLY GOOD."

TACT IN OFFICIATING IS NOT SAYING WHAT YOU ARE WANTING TO SAY TO A COACH WHEN YOU SHOULDN'T.

JOHN C LAURIE

IF YOU "BLOW" THE BIGGEST CALL OF THE GAME AND YOU BELIEVE THE WORLD IS AGAINST YOU, DON'T FORGET THERE ARE A FEW COUNTRIES THAT ARE STILL NEUTRAL.

IT IS OKAY TO HAVE A "GUT FEELING" WHILE OFFICIATING BUT NEVER BELIEVE THAT IT IS ENOUGH.

JOHN C LAURIE

IT IS IMPOSSIBLE TO OFFICIATE A PERFECT GAME BUT IT IS POSSIBLE TO DEMONSTRATE A PERFECTION OF CHARACTER AND INTEGRITY THROUGHOUT THE GAME.

AN EFFECTIVE REFEREE ALWAYS DEMONSTRATES OPTIMISM THROUGHOUT THE GAME.

JOHN C LAURIE

YOUR OFFICIATING CAREER, WHETHER IT HAS BEEN GOOD OR BAD, IS LIKE A LARGE ROLL OF TOILET PAPER. THE CLOSER YOU GET TO THE END, THE FASTER IT GOES.

THE STRONGEST REFEREES (LEADERS) OF FOOTBALL CREWS HAVE A TENDENCY TO MAKE THE LEAST NOISE.

JOHN C LAURIE

SMART OFFICIALS KNOW HOW TO PLAY DUMB WHEN CONFRONTED BY A COACH ACTING DUMB AND SMART WHEN CONVERSING WITH A SMART COACH.

THE BEST OFFICIALS PROFIT FROM THEIR EXPERIENCE AND THEIR MISTAKES; POOR OFFICIALS PROFIT FROM NEITHER.

JOHN C LAURIE

PRIDE IS AN INTERESTING QUALITY FOR OFFICIALS. TOO MUCH PRIDE CAN MAKE AN OFFICIAL APPEAR RIDICULOUS; TOO LITTLE KEEPS HIM FROM SUCCESS.

DURING A WELL-OFFICIATED FOOTBALL GAME YOU WILL LOSE A FEW BATTLES IN ORDER TO WIN THE WAR.

JOHN C LAURIE

FOR EVERY DIFFICULT ACTION TAKEN BY OFFICIALS ON THE FIELD, THERE IS AN EQUAL AND OPPOSITE CRITICISM FROM HALF OF THE FANS WATCHING THE GAME.

A CREW DOESN'T HAVE TO LOOK BUSY IF THEY USE THE CORRECT BALL MECHANICS THE FIRST TIME.

JOHN C LAURIE

AS AN OFFICIAL YOU WILL HAVE ENEMIES. THE KEY IS HOW YOU DEAL WITH THEM AS THEY WILL EITHER HELP YOUR PROMOTION OR SPEED UP YOUR DEMOTION.

THERE ARE TIMES IN A FOOTBALL GAME WHEN THERE ARE NO SOLUTIONS—SO SIMPLY ADMIRE THE PROBLEM.

JOHN C LAURIE

WHEN IT IS TIME FOR THE CREW TO SORT THROUGH PROBLEMS ON THE FIELD, REMEMBER THAT EVERYONE HAS MORE INFORMATION THAN ANYONE.

IF AS A REFEREE YOUR CREW IS ALWAYS WORKING IN CRISIS MANAGEMENT, YOU ARE NOT A GOOD MANAGER OF THE GAME.

JOHN C LAURIE

THE BEST REFEREES ADAPT THEIR LEADERSHIP STYLE TO FIT THE MULTIPLE SITUATIONS THAT OCCUR DURING THE GAME.

OFFICIALS WITH DISCRETION HAVE THE QUALITY OF KNOWING THE BETTER PART OF INDISCRETION.

JOHN C LAURIE

WHEN THE GAME YOU ARE OFFICIATING SPEAKS FOR ITSELF, DON'T INTERRUPT IT TO SHOW YOUR "CONTROL" OR "PRESENCE."

THE BEST CREWS SEEM TO BE ABLE TO JUMP INTO TROUBLED WATERS AND NOT MAKE A SPLASH.

JOHN C LAURIE

SOMETIMES DURING A VERY DIFFICULT SITUATION, THE ONLY REAL CHOICE ONE HAS AS AN OFFICIAL IS TO REMAIN IN CHARGE OF HIS ATTITUDE ABOUT THE SITUATION.

IF YOUR SOLUTION TO A PROBLEM ON THE FIELD POSES NEW PROBLEMS, YOU HAVEN'T FOUND THE RIGHT SOLUTION.

JOHN C LAURIE

IN ORDER TO BE A SUCCESSFUL OFFICIAL, YOUR DEDICATION TO BEING SUCCESSFUL MUST BE GREATER THAN YOUR FEAR OF FAILING.

IF YOU THINK LITTLE OF A COACH OR ANOTHER OFFICIAL, YOU SHOULD SAY AS LITTLE AS YOU THINK.

JOHN C LAURIE

OFFICIALS IMPROVE WITH EXPERIENCE BUT IT IS THE CAPACITY TO DEAL WITH EXPERIENCES AND IMPROVE THAT MAKES THE BIGGEST DIFFERENCE IN OFFICIALS.

SIMPLY PUT, THINGS TURN OUT BEST FOR THE CREWS WHO MAKE THE BEST OF THE WAY THINGS TURN OUT.

JOHN C LAURIE

YOU CAN MEASURE THE STRENGTH OF AN OFFICIAL BY DETERMINING HOW HE RECOVERS FROM A SERIES OF "LITTLE THINGS" GOING WRONG.

THE CLOCK ON THE SCOREBOARD KEEPS EVERYTHING FROM HAPPENING AT ONCE.

JOHN C LAURIE

IF YOU HAVE A COMPLICATED PROBLEM TO SOLVE ON THE FIELD, TRY APPROACHING A GOOD SOLUTION FROM A DIFFERENT POINT OF VIEW.

A GOOD WAY TO AVOID STEPPING ON A COACH'S TOES IS TO TRY BRIEFLY TO GET INTO HIS SHOES.

JOHN C LAURIE

GOOD OFFICIALS DON'T HAVE NEGATIVE THOUGHTS AFTER THE GAME. IF THINGS WERE GOOD, IT WAS GREAT; IF THINGS WERE BAD, IT WAS EXPERIENCE.

IN DEALING WITH AN IRATE COACH
THERE IS A FINE LINE BETWEEN BEING
"BIG" AND BELITTLING HIM.

JOHN C LAURIE

THE FASTEST WAY TO GET RELIEF FROM
A GAME THAT HAS GOTTEN OUT OF
CONTROL IS TO SIMPLY FIND WAYS TO
"SLOW IT DOWN."

IT IS OKAY TO COPY THE STRENGTHS OF OTHER OFFICIALS BUT MAKE YOUR OWN IMPRESSIONS.

JOHN C LAURIE

YOU EITHER PLAN TO WORK A GREAT GAME OR YOU PLAN NOT TO WORK A BAD GAME. THIS IS THE KEY DIFFERENCE BETWEEN SUCCESS AND MEDIOCRITY.

EXCELLENCE BEGINS WHEN YOU ASK
FOR AND EXPECT MORE OF YOURSELF
THAN ANYONE ELSE ON THE CREW DOES.

JOHN C LAURIE

A HOLE AND CONCENTRATION ARE BOTH
INVISIBLE, BUT THE FORMER CAN BREAK
YOUR NECK AND THE LATTER YOUR
CAREER.

OFFICIATING PRESENCE IS MUCH MORE THAN BEING ON THE FIELD.

JOHN C LAURIE

THE SECOND HALF OF YOUR OFFICIATING CAREER IS MADE UP OF HABITS ACQUIRED DURING THE FIRST HALF SO START WITH GOOD MECHANICS.

IT IS IMPOSSIBLE TO REACH YOUR HIGHEST LEVEL AS AN OFFICIAL WITHOUT OVERCOMING ADVERSITY.

JOHN C LAURIE

OFFICIATING IS A GAME OF ANTICIPATION, RECOGNITION AND THEN DOING THE RIGHT THING.

PHOTO COMPOSITE BY RICHARD WHITENBURG, UMPIRE

One of my favorite photos which is a tribute to a special friend
and great Back Judge, Poncho Girard (lower right), was taken one
month before his untimely death.

SAY WHAT YOU HAVE TO SAY TO A COACH
NOT WHAT YOU WOULD LIKE TO SAY.

JOHN C LAURIE

UNTIL THERE IS A NEED TO ANTICIPATE
POSSIBLE CONSEQUENCES IN THE TENSE
PART OF THE GAME, MOST ZEBRAS WILL
LOOK SOMEWHAT ALIKE.

PREVIOUS MISTAKES FURNISH THE BEST MATERIAL WITH WHICH TO BUILD TOWARD A SUCCESSFUL CAREER.

JOHN C LAURIE

MISTAKES IN OFFICIATING CAN BE BRIDGES BETWEEN INEXPERIENCE AND WISDOM; DON'T BURN THEM.

YOU CAN'T BECOME A BETTER OFFICIAL REMAINING WHO YOU ARE.

JOHN C LAURIE

THE LAW OF PROBABILITY IN OFFICIATING IS MORE ACCURATE WITH GENERAL PRINCIPLES AND SITUATIONS AND NOT AS EFFECTIVE WITH SPECIFIC OCCURRENCES.

A GREAT DEAL OF WHAT AN OFFICIAL SEES ON A PLAY DEPENDS ON WHAT HE IS LOOKING FOR.

JOHN C LAURIE

THE BEST CREWS MAKE MISTAKES WHICH ARE UNDERSTOOD AND FORGIVEN BUT NOT DISLOYALTY.

IT TAKES A LOOSE REIN FOR A REFEREE TO KEEP HIS CREW TIGHT.

JOHN C LAURIE

THE BEST OFFICIALS USE HALF AS MANY WORDS TO COMMUNICATE WITH A COACH EFFECTIVELY AS A POOR OFFICIAL.

THE GREATEST REVENGE YOU CAN HAVE IS TO FORGIVE A COACH FOR BEING A JERK.

JOHN C LAURIE

TO BE ABSOLUTELY CERTAIN ABOUT A RULE INTERPRETATION, YOU MUST KNOW ABSOLUTELY EVERYTHING OR NOTHING ABOUT IT.

A GOOD REFEREE DOES NOT ALLOW HIS CREW TO DICTATE HIS CONSCIENCE.

JOHN C LAURIE

IF IT TAKES A LOT OF WORDS TO EXPLAIN A SITUATION TO A COACH OR WHEN USING YOUR MIC, GIVE IT MORE THOUGHT.

THE BEST WAY TO UNDERSTANDING A COACH IS TO CONSIDER THINGS FROM HIS POINT OF VIEW.

JOHN C LAURIE

A GOOD OFFICIAL WILL FIRST LEARN THE GAME AND, WITH EXPERIENCE, HE WILL UNDERSTAND THE GAME.

IF YOUR CREW IS AGREEING WITH
EVERYTHING YOU ARE THINKING, YOU
ARE THE ONLY ONE DOING THE THINKING.

JOHN C LAURIE

TAKE EVERY PLAY OF EVERY GAME
SERIOUSLY BUT NOT ANY PLAY OR ANY
GAME IS CAREER ENDING.

FOOTBALL NEEDS A RULE BOOK; GOOD OFFICIALS WITH INTEGRITY DON'T NEED RULES.

JOHN C LAURIE

THE KEY TO BECOMING A SUCCESSFUL OFFICIAL IS TO WORK TO BECOME A BETTER ONE AND NOT TO ACQUIRE SOMETHING IN OFFICIATING.

THE BEST OFFICIALS TALK VERY LITTLE ABOUT THEMSELVES.

JOHN C LAURIE

IF YOU OFFICIATE A GREAT GAME, ACT AS IF YOU ARE USED TO IT. IF YOU HAVE A POOR GAME, CHALLENGE YOURSELF TO MAKE THE NEXT ONE BETTER.

THE BEST OFFICIALS HAVE THE ABILITY TO CONCEAL THEIR ABILITY WHILE OFFICIATING DIFFICULT GAMES.

JOHN C LAURIE

BEWARE OF THE COACH THAT FALSELY LOSES HIS TEMPER TO SEE IF YOU WILL LOSE YOURS.

ALWAYS PUT OFF TO THE NEXT GAME A CALL THAT YOU SHOULDN'T MAKE.

JOHN C LAURIE

IF YOU OFFICIATE WHAT YOU THINK WAS A GREAT GAME AND HAD NO AGGRAVATION, YOU PROBABLY MISSED A FEW THINGS.

IT IS NOT SO MUCH WHAT AN
OFFICIAL KNOWS BUT HOW HE USES
WHAT HE KNOWS.

JOHN C LAURIE

THE REFEREE WITH THE BEST CREW
WILL ALWAYS FIND A WAY TO CATCH
OFFICIALS DURING THE GAMES AND
RECOGNIZE THEM FOR THEIR EFFORT.
POSITIVE REINFORCEMENT ALWAYS
BRINGS POSITIVE RESULTS.

THE HARDER YOU WORK TO BECOME A
BETTER OFFICIAL THE LESS YOU WILL
CALL IT WORK.

JOHN C LAURIE

IN DEALING WITH A COMPLEX SITUATION
DURING THE GAME, BE CAREFUL NOT TO
PREJUDGE YOUR OPTIONS UNTIL YOU
HAVE ALL THE INFORMATION.

GOOD OFFICIALS KEEP THEIR EYES WIDE
OPEN AND THEIR EARS HALF CLOSED
DURING THE GAME.

JOHN C LAURIE

IF THE COACH IS RIGHT AND YOU ARE
WRONG, DON'T LET HIM BEAT YOU WITH
POLITENESS.

IT IS OKAY TO HEAR A COACH WHO IS
YELLING AT YOU BUT TO ONLY LISTEN
WHEN HE IS TALKING TO YOU.

JOHN C LAURIE

OFFICIATING SUCCESS IS MORE A
FUNCTION OF CONSISTENT COMMON
SENSE THAN ANY OTHER FACTOR.

ALL OF THE BEST OFFICIALS DEMONSTRATE A GREAT DEAL OF PRIDE IN WHAT THEY DO.

JOHN C LAURIE

ALL OFFICIALS MAKE MISTAKES. GOOD OFFICIALS LEARN FROM THEM; THE BEST OFFICIALS GAIN CONFIDENCE AND THE COURAGE TO MAKE NEW MISTAKES.

THE BEST VISION AN OFFICIAL CAN HAVE BEFORE THE SNAP IS INSIGHT.

JOHN C LAURIE

THE TRUE ART OF PATIENCE AMONG OFFICIALS IS THE ABILITY TO PUT UP WITH ANY IRATE COACH WHEN IT WOULD BE EASY TO PUT HIM DOWN.

A NICE COMPLIMENT FOR AN OFFICIAL:
"HE IS ENTHUSIASTIC AND KEEPS
HIS COOL."

JOHN C LAURIE

OFFICIALS WITH GREAT AMBITIONS
MAKE A HABIT OF NOT MISSING THE
SMALL THINGS.

WHEN THERE IS A "DETOUR" IN THE GAME, THE GOOD CREWS TAKE THE HIGHER ROAD.

JOHN C LAURIE

A GOOD SIGN OF A MATURE COACH IS ONE WHO REALIZES THAT HE NOT ONLY HAS THE RIGHT TO BE RIGHT BUT ALSO TO BE WRONG.

MODESTY IS THE T-SHIRT YOU WEAR UNDER YOUR GAME SHIRT.

JOHN C LAURIE

HAVING FOCUS AND TAKING OFFICIATING SERIOUSLY IS THE DIFFERENCE BETWEEN EXPERIENCING AND GAINING EXPERIENCE.

A HANDFUL OF COMMON SENSE IS WORTH AN ARM LOAD OF RULE BOOKS.

JOHN C LAURIE

GOOD OFFICIALS DEMONSTRATE PROPER DISCRETION BY HIDING THINGS THAT HAVE NO REMEDY OR FAIRNESS.

THE BEST WAY TO REMAIN THE BEST REFEREE IN THE CONFERENCE IS TO WORK SMARTER THAN #2.

JOHN C LAURIE

KNOWING HOW TO BE BIG AND NOT TO BELITTLE IS AN IMPORTANT PART OF BEING AN EFFECTIVE REFEREE.

AN OFFICIAL'S REPUTATION IS
DETERMINED BY DESIRING TO ACHIEVE
AT THE HIGHEST LEVEL AND THEN
DOING IT.

JOHN C LAURIE

DON'T GET EXCITED ABOUT YOUR "GOOD
CALL" AS THE FANS MAKE THE SAME
AMOUNT OF NOISE IF THEY WANT TO
HANG YOU.

THE BEST WAY TO IMPROVE THE ABILITY OF AN OFFICIAL IS TO IMPROVE HIS CONFIDENCE.

JOHN C LAURIE

GENERALLY THE FIRST STEP IN SOLVING THE PROBLEM IS FOR SOMEONE ON THE CREW TO TELL THE REFEREE.

A DIFFICULT GAME TO OFFICIATE DOESN'T NEED TO BE A LONG GAME IF YOU TAKE IT ONE SNAP AT A TIME.

JOHN C LAURIE

TWO WAYS TO SHORTEN YOUR CAREER AS AN OFFICIAL: UNDERRATE OTHER OFFICIALS AND OVERRATE YOUR OWN ABILITIES.

COURAGE/WEAKNESS, HERO/COWARD, RIGHT/WRONG: ALL DETERMINED BY A PENALTY FLAG OR A WHISTLE.

JOHN C LAURIE

TALKING TO AN IRATE COACH IS LIKE SOMEONE TRYING TO SADDLE A COW. YOU WORK HARD TO DO IT, BUT WHAT IS THE POINT?

DIFFICULT GAMES THAT YOU OFFICIATE SUCCESSFULLY DEVELOP CHARACTER AS WELL AS YOUR CAREER.

JOHN C LAURIE

TELL ME THE OFFICIALS YOU RESPECT IN THE CONFERENCE AND I WILL KNOW WHAT KIND OF MAN YOU ARE.

AN OFFICIAL'S ABILITY TO LOOK INSIDE HIMSELF ALLOWS OTHERS TO SEE HIM MORE CLEARLY.

JOHN C LAURIE

THE BEST TIME TO REPENT AN INADVERTENT WHISTLE IS BEFORE THE WHISTLE IS BLOWN.

IF YOU WANT TO KNOW HOW FAR AN OFFICIAL IS HEADED UP OR DOWN IN HIS CAREER, STUDY HIS EXCUSES.

JOHN C LAURIE

DETERMINING THE BEST CAREER AN OFFICIAL CAN HAVE IS LIKE ROLLING A SNOWBALL—THE FURTHER IT IS ROLLED, THE MORE IT GAINS.

ADVERSITY INTRODUCES GOOD AND POOR OFFICIALS TO THEMSELVES.

JOHN C LAURIE

A FOOTBALL GAME EXPOSES EITHER COURAGE OR FEAR IN AN OFFICIAL. BY CHOOSING COURAGE HE IS IN FOR AN EXCITING AND EXHILARATING RIDE THAT NOT ONLY LASTS LONGER BUT IS ACTUALLY EASIER TO ACCOMPLISH.

IT IS GOOD TO REMEMBER THAT EVEN
THE BEST OFFICIALS ARE FOOLED ONCE
IN A WHILE.

JOHN C LAURIE

A FEW OFFICIALS BECOME SUCCESSFUL
BECAUSE THEY ARE DESTINED; MOST DO
BECAUSE THEY ARE DETERMINED.

THE KEY TO OFFICIATING "BIG GAMES" SUCCESSFULLY IS TO STAY IN CONTROL OF THE NON-OBVIOUS PARTS OF THE GAME.

JOHN C LAURIE

I HAVE NEVER MET A WELL-DISCIPLINED OFFICIAL WHOSE OFFICIATING CAREER WAS A FAILURE.

BECOMING A BETTER OFFICIAL ISN'T WORK UNLESS YOU WOULD RATHER BE SOMETHING ELSE.

JOHN C LAURIE

SOME REFEREES ARE LIKE DIRECTIONAL SIGNS POINTING THE RIGHT WAY IN THE PREGAME BUT LATER NEVER GOING THAT WAY ON THE FIELD.

IT IS EASIER TO BUILD AN OFFICIATING CAREER THAN TO MAINTAIN IT.

JOHN C LAURIE

REASON AND COMMON SENSE ARE GOOD APPLICATIONS WHEN THE SITUATION IS NOT IN THE RULE BOOK.

THE MARK OF SUCCESS FOR AN
EXEMPLARY OFFICIAL IS WHEN HE NO
LONGER FEARS FAILURE.

JOHN C LAURIE

THE BEST OFFICIALS USE THEIR ABILITIES
AND AUTHORITY WHEN THEY CAN AND
TAKE THE REST AS IT HAPPENS.

THE DIFFERENCE BETWEEN NEARLY RIGHT AND EXACTLY RIGHT IS A BOWL WATCH OR WATCHING THE GAME ON TV.

JOHN C LAURIE

DON'T OFFER ADVICE TO OTHER OFFICIALS THAT HAS NOT BEEN SUCCESSFUL IN YOUR OWN PERFORMANCE.

A GOOD FOOTBALL CREW COMES TOGETHER, STAYS TOGETHER AND WORKS TOGETHER!

JOHN C LAURIE

FOURTH AND GOAL AT THE TWO-YARD LINE . . . LUCK IS BEING READY FOR THE CHANCE TO MAKE THE RIGHT CALL.

THERE IS NO GREATER GIFT THE REFEREE CAN GIVE HIS CREW THAN FOR EACH ONE OF THEM TO FEEL APPRECIATED.

JOHN C LAURIE

IF YOU DON'T WORK THE GAMES YOU WANT, THINK ABOUT THE ONES YOU DON'T GET THAT YOU DIDN'T WANT.

EVERYTHING YOU WANT TO SAY TO A COACH BECOMES A LITTLE DIFFERENT WHEN YOU SAY IT OUT LOUD.

JOHN C LAURIE

THE DIFFERENCE BETWEEN A GOOD AND GREAT OFFICIAL IS THAT THE GREAT ONES CAN ALSO TEACH WHAT THEY KNOW.

THE SECRET OF SUCCESSFUL
FOOTBALL CREWS IS THEIR
CONSISTENCY TO PURPOSE.

JOHN C LAURIE

IT IS NOT THE ONE WHO SCORES
HIGHEST ON THE RULES TEST BUT
THE OFFICIAL WITH COURAGE WHO
UNDERSTANDS THE GAME OF FOOTBALL
THAT WILL HAVE THE DISTINGUISHED
OFFICIATING CAREER.

CHANCE FAVORS THE OFFICIAL WHO HUSTLES.

JOHN C LAURIE

ALL OFFICIALS BECOME DISCOURAGED FROM TIME TO TIME. A GOOD OFFICIAL DOES NOT BECOME A POOR OFFICIAL UNTIL HE BLAMES OTHERS AND STOPS TRYING.

THE KEY TO A SUCCESSFUL OFFICIATING CAREER IS TO HAVE JUST UNDER THE BAGGAGE LIMIT.

JOHN C LAURIE

IF YOU ARE INVOLVED IN A GAME THAT HAS AN INADVERTENT WHISTLE, CREMATE IT—DON'T EMBALM IT.

THREE PARTS OF OFFICIATING SUCCESS: 1) WORK HARD, 2) DON'T QUIT, 3) USE COMMON SENSE.

JOHN C LAURIE

UNDERSTANDING WHAT YOU DON'T KNOW ABOUT RULES IS JUST AS IMPORTANT AS WHAT YOU DO KNOW.

IF YOU WANT A COACH TO LISTEN TO YOU, LET HIM TALK.

JOHN C LAURIE

SUCCESSFUL FOOTBALL OFFICIALS WORK THROUGH THEIR MISTAKES AND FAILURES ON THE FIELD WITHOUT LOSING THEIR ENTHUSIUASM TO OFFICIATE.

GOOD CREWS HAVE THE LUCK OF HAVING
GOOD TALENT AND THEY ALSO HAVE THE
TALENT FOR LUCK.

JOHN C LAURIE

OFFICIALS ON THEIR WAY UP OR DOWN
CANNOT FIND A BETTER SPARRING
PARTNER THAN ADVERSITY.

OBSTACLES YOU OVER COME DURING A DIFFICULT-TO-OFFICIATE GAME ARE THE PATH TO FUTURE SUCCESSES.

JOHN C LAURIE

YOU LEARN SOMETHING IN EVERY FOOTBALL GAME YOU OFFICIATE AND SOMETIMES WHAT YOU LEARN IS THAT LAST WEEK YOU DID IT WRONG.

THE BEST OFFICIALS ARE YOUNG AT HEART.

JOHN C LAURIE

A REFEREE WHO IS A GOOD COMMUNICATOR WHEN VISITING WITH A COACH ABOUT THE "FACTS" OF A SITUATION CAN PERSUADE A COACH WITH A TOTALLY DIFFERENT POINT OF VIEW THAT THERE MAY BE TWO SIDES TO THE ISSUE, AND THAT HE IS PROBABLY WRONG, BUT VIDEO WILL MAKE THE FINAL DECISION LATER.

YOU DON'T PRACTICE OFFICIATING SPRING GAMES; OFFICIATE THEM.

JOHN C LAURIE

A GOOD OFFICIAL LEARNS TO BREAK THE BAD HABIT OF "WORRY" BY DECIDING HE CAN MASTER THE WORST THING THAT CAN HAPPEN TO HIM IN A GAME.

A GOOD WAY TO RECOGNIZE AN EXCELLENT CREW IS THAT THEY ARE RARELY SURPRISED BY ANYTHING.

JOHN C LAURIE

THE BEST GOAL OF A GOOD CREW IS TO HAVE COLLECTIVELY FEWER MISTAKES EACH WEEK OF THE SEASON.

THE MOST EFFECTIVE ANSWER YOU CAN GIVE A COACH IS THE ONE WHICH DESTROYS HIS QUESTION.

JOHN C LAURIE

OFFICIATING MISTAKES ARE EITHER THE BRIDGE BETWEEN INEXPERIENCE AND IMPROVEMENT OR A SHORT CAREER.

THE BEST OFFICIALS DON'T JUST SEE PROBLEMS, THEY BRING SOLUTIONS TO PROBLEMS.

JOHN C LAURIE

BEWARE OF THE CREW WHERE EVERYONE WANTS TO BE CHIEF AND NO ONE WANTS TO BE BRAVE.

DON'T INSULT YOUR OFFICIATING
INTELLIGENCE BY ALWAYS BELIEVING
WHAT A COACH JUST SAID ABOUT YOU.

JOHN C LAURIE

THE MOST DIFFICULT DECISION AN
OFFICIAL WILL MAKE IN HIS CAREER IS
THE DECISION TO RETIRE.

THE BEST WAY TO IMPROVE YOUR OFFICIATING SKILLS IS TO COMPETE WITH YOURSELF, NOT ANOTHER OFFICIAL.

JOHN C LAURIE

THERE IS NO "ORIGINAL MISTAKE" IN OFFICIATING A FOOTBALL GAME. RELAX; YOURS WASN'T THE FIRST AND IT WILL BE REPEATED.

THE BEST OFFICIALS ENJOY THEIR CAREERS WITHOUT COMPARING THEM TO OTHERS.

JOHN C LAURIE

BEING RECOGNIZED AS AN EXCELLENT OFFICIAL IS ACHIEVED THROUGH GAINING EXPERIENCE AND NOT REPEATING MISTAKES. ADD PERSISTENCE AND YOU HAVE THE FORMULA FOR AN EXCELLENT CAREER IN OFFICIATING.

NO OFFICIAL BELOW YOUR LEVEL SHOULD INTIMIDATE YOU AND NO ONE YOUR EQUAL WOULD.

JOHN C LAURIE

THE BEST WAY FOR A COACH TO WIN AN ARGUMENT IS TO BE RIGHT. THE ONLY WAY FOR THE OFFICIAL TO LOSE IS TO CONTINUE TO ARGUE!

MISTAKES WILL HAPPEN. IT IS BETTER TO MAKE ONE OF ACTION THAN INACTION.

JOHN C LAURIE

GOOD REFEREES WILL TELL THE CREW WHAT TO EXPECT, AND THE BEST ONES WILL RAISE THE LEVEL OF EXPECTATION OF EACH CREW MEMBER.

THERE IS A BIG DIFFERENCE BETWEEN UNDERSTANDING THE RULE BOOK AND KNOWING THE GAME.

JOHN C LAURIE

CLEAR THOUGHT AND DISCUSSION IN AN EFFECTIVE PREGAME IS SIMPLY A REHEARSAL FOR THINGS TO COME.

A GOOD CREW WILL TAKE THEIR
WORK ON THE FIELD SERIOUSLY BUT
THEMSELVES LIGHTLY.

JOHN C LAURIE

SOME REFEREES RUN INTO PROBLEMS
WHEN THEY TRY TO PUT A FAMILIAR
SOLUTION TO THE WRONG PROBLEM.

THE SIGN OF A GOOD CREW IS THAT THEY RESPECT YOU IN SPITE OF YOUR PERSONAL ACHIEVEMENTS.

JOHN C LAURIE

IF YOU WANT TO CRITICIZE YOUR CREW, A GOOD PRACTICE STARTS IN FRONT OF A MIRROR.

WHEN A THOUGHT IS TOO WEAK TO EXPLAIN TO A COACH, IT IS BEST TO SIMPLY DROP IT.

JOHN C LAURIE

THE BEST OFFICIALS WILL MAKE MORE OPPORTUNITIES THAN THOSE THAT SIMPLY FIND THEM.

A WINNING COMBINATION TO BECOME A GOOD OFFICIAL: COMMON SENSE, COOLNESS AND ENTHUSIASM.

JOHN C LAURIE

THE BEST OFFICIALS HAVE THE ABILITY TO DO THE THINGS THEY NEED TO DO AT THE RIGHT TIME, WHETHER THEY WANT TO OR NOT.

THE BEST WAY TO DEVELOP SELF-CONFIDENCE IS TO BE PREPARED.

JOHN C LAURIE

KEEP IN MIND THAT THE PROBLEMS YOU PASS ON THINKING THAT THEY WILL GO AWAY BY THEMSELVES USUALLY COME BACK BY THEMSEVES.

A GOOD REASON NOT TO ARGUE WITH
A COACH IS THAT USUALLY HIS JOB
DEPENDS ON NOT BEING CONVINCED.

JOHN C LAURIE

THE CHARACTER OF AN OFFICIAL IS
OFTEN DEMONSTRATED IN "BIG" GAMES.
IT WAS MADE IN THE "SMALL" GAMES
EARLIER IN HIS CAREER.

GOOD OFFICIATING CREWS ARE A CHOICE AND DON'T DEPEND ON CHANCE.

JOHN C LAURIE

IF YOU COULD KICK THE CREW MEMBER IN YOUR CREW MOST RESPONSIBLE FOR YOUR MISTAKES, YOU COULDN'T SIT DOWN IN THE POST-GAME MEETING WITH THE SUPERVISOR.

DON'T MISS A CHANCE TO BE RIGHT WHILE OFFICIATING JUST BECAUSE SOMETHING ELSE IS MORE CONVENIENT.

JOHN C LAURIE

MORE THAN ONE CREW CHIEF (REFEREE) IN A CREW WILL EVENTUALLY CAUSE THE GROUP TO FAIL FOR LACK OF UNITY.

IF YOU WANT TO KNOW WHAT AN
OFFICIAL THINKS OF HIMSELF, LISTEN TO
HOW HE DESCRIBES OTHERS.

JOHN C LAURIE

BE CAREFUL OF OVERUSING YOUR
AUTHORITY WITH YOUR CREW OR THE
HEAD COACH. THE MORE YOU USE, THE
LESS YOU HAVE

YOUR CAREER IS IN THE HANDS OF A COACH WHEN YOU LOSE YOUR TEMPER.

JOHN C LAURIE

IF THE REFEREE WANTS HIS CREW TO KEEP THEIR FEET ON THE GROUND DURING THE GAME, PUT SOME RESPONSIBILITIES ON THEIR SHOULDERS.

OFFICIATING TALENT IS NOT DEVELOPED
OVERNIGHT BUT IT IS SOMETIMES
RECOGNIZED OVERNIGHT.

JOHN C LAURIE

DON'T CONSIDER YOURSELF AN
"EXPERIENCED" OFFICIAL UNTIL YOU
HAVE MANAGED DURING THE GAME AN
UNSOLVABLE PROBLEM.

GENERALLY THE CREW WILL GROW OR
FALL INDIVIDUALLY AND COLLECTIVELY
AS THE REFEREE BELIEVES IN THEM.

JOHN C LAURIE

HALF THE BATTLE OF GETTING THROUGH
A TOUGH GAME IS TO KEEP YOUR FEET
ON THE GROUND—BUT YOU ALSO HAVE
TO KEEP YOUR FEET MOVING.

AN OFFICIAL'S NEAT, CLEAN, WELL-PRESSED UNIFORM KEEPS HIM FROM LOOKING HARD PRESSED.

JOHN C LAURIE

CREW PROBLEMS ARE SIMPLY MESSAGES. GOOD CREWS READ THEM ACCURATELY AND MAKE APPROPRIATE CHANGES.

THE POSITION OF REFEREE DOES NOT CONFER POWER BUT IMPOSES RESPONSIBILITY.

JOHN C LAURIE

A DIFFICULT LESSON FOR ANY GOOD OFFICIAL OR LEADER IS THAT NOT EVERYONE WISHES YOU SUCCESS.

GOOD FOOTBALL MECHANICS ARE A
BAD CRUTCH BUT AN EXCELLENT
WALKING STICK.

JOHN C LAURIE

AFTER ALL OF THE FACTS HAVE BEEN
PRESENTED TO THE REFEREE DURING
A CREW CONFERENCE, AT LEAST ONE
OFFICIAL NEEDS TO MAKE SURE THE
OBVIOUS HAS NOT BEEN OVERLOOKED.

THE BEST REFEREES ELIMINATE THE NON-ESSENTIALS IN THE PREGAME.

JOHN C LAURIE

THE DIFFERENCE BETWEEN A GOOD AND POOR REFEREE IS HOW HE USES HIS ERASER WITH A CREW. ONE RUBS MISTAKES OUT; THE OTHER RUBS THEM IN.

THE FINAL PLATEAU OF OFFICIATING SUCCESS LIES WITHIN THE OFFICIAL AND NOT THE GAME.

JOHN C LAURIE

AFTER YOU LEARN THE RULE BOOK, GOOD OFFICIALS STEP UP BY LEARNING HOW TO LEARN FROM THE GAME ON THE FIELD.

WHEN A CREW CONFERENCE LEAVES THE REFEREE IN DOUBT, DO THE CONVENTIONAL THING.

JOHN C LAURIE

SOMETIMES DURING A GAME IT IS DIFFICULT TO SEE A CLEAR DECISION AND YOU MUST SIMPLY TAKE THE LEAST BLURRED.

ASSUMPTIONS ARE THE TERMITES
THAT RUIN THE FOUNDATION SET IN THE
PREGAME.

JOHN C LAURIE

IN ORDER TO BECOME A SUCCESSFUL
OFFICIAL, YOU ARE EITHER GIVEN A
CHANCE OR YOU TAKE A CHANCE.

WHAT SEPARATES A "BOOK" OFFICIAL
FROM A GREAT OFFICIAL IS THE
DIFFERENCE BETWEEN KNOWLEDGE
AND WISDOM.

JOHN C LAURIE

JUST LIKE IN ANYTHING, TIMING IS
EVERYTHING. THINKING TOO LONG
ABOUT DOING SOMETHING CAN BE
ITS UNDOING.

A MAJOR DIFFERENCE BETWEEN GOOD
AND BAD OFFICIALS IS HOW THEY VIEW
THEIR MISTAKES.

JOHN C LAURIE

BE CAREFUL HOW YOU USE THE WORD
"HATE" AS AN OFFICIAL. IT IS OKAY TO
HATE WHAT A COACH DOES OR HOW HE
ACTS, BUT YOU PERSONALLY LOSE WHEN
YOU PERSONALLY HATE.

THE ABILITY TO LEAD A CREW AS A REFEREE IS AN ATTITUDE BEFORE IT IS ABILITY.

JOHN C LAURIE

THE BEST OFFICIALS OVERCOME REAL DIFFICULTIES THAT OCCUR DURING THE GAME; THE POOR ONES GET STUCK ON THE INCONSEQUENTIAL ONES.

THE APPROPRIATE TIME TO DO THE PROPER THING IN OFFICIATING IS BEFORE YOU ARE REQUIRED TO DO IT.

JOHN C LAURIE

DURING A CREW CONFERENCE ON A COMPLICATED PLAY, BEWARE OF THE HALF TRUTH AS YOU MAY GET THE WRONG HALF.

IF YOUR COMPETENT CREW DOES NOT SHOW ON THE FIELD, IT IS THE SAME AS INCOMPETENCE.

JOHN C LAURIE

WHICH CREW WOULD A GOOD REFEREE WANT: ONE THAT WORKED FOR HIM OR ONE THAT WORKED WITH HIM?

LITTLE THINGS IN A FOOTBALL GAME BRING PERFECTION AND PERFECTION IS NO LITTLE THING.

JOHN C LAURIE

OFFICIALS WHO VALUE THEIR PRIVILEGE AS A DIVISION I REFEREE ABOVE THE HIGH CHARACTER AND INTEGRITY EXPECTED, LOSE ALL THREE.

THE RULE BOOK IS IMPORTANT BUT INTEGRITY NEEDS NO RULES.

JOHN C LAURIE

WHEN YOU THINK ABOUT THE BEST OFFICIALS, THEY SIMPLY DO ALL THAT THEY CAN DO. APPLY THE RULES OF THE GAME FAIRLY. THIS IS IMPOSSIBLE FOR POOR OFFICIALS TO DO.

THE BEST REFEREES CAN GIVE A TROUBLED OFFICIAL A SHOT IN THE ARM WITHOUT FEELING THE NEEDLE.

JOHN C LAURIE

ACCEPTING SUGGESTIONS AND CRITICISM, REMAINING POSITIVE AND STRIVING TO IMPROVE IS THE RECIPE FOR SUCCESS.

EVERY FIVE YEARS THE BEST OFFICIALS MUST RELEARN THE OFFICIATING GAME.

JOHN C LAURIE

IF A COACH IMMEDIATELY SAYS TO YOU AFTER A VERY DIFFICULT PLAY, "THERE IS A GOOD CHANCE YOU GOT IT RIGHT," THERE IS A GOOD CHANCE YOU GOT IT WRONG.

IF THE REFEREE'S CAREER REACHES A POINT WHERE HE STOPS LEARNING, HE ALSO STOPS LEADING.

JOHN C LAURIE

THE BEST OFFICIALS SHOW PRESENCE ON THE FIELD. POOR OFFICIALS THINK THAT SIMPLY BEING THERE IS ENOUGH.

THE ONE THING EVERY OFFICIAL CAN
ACHIEVE WITHOUT FAILURE IS GIVING
GREAT EFFORT.

JOHN C LAURIE

IT IS NOT THE CREW THAT MAKES THE
"GAME OF THE CENTURY," BUT THE
"GAME OF THE CENTURY" THAT ALLOWS
THE PERCEPTION OF A GREAT CREW.

IF YOU ARE IN AN ARGUMENT WITH A COACH, THE FIRST THING YOU SHOULD DO IS APOLOGIZE.

JOHN C LAURIE

THE BEST REFEREE HAS THE ABILITY TO MAKE HIMSELF PROGRESSIVELY UNNECESSARY TO HIS CREW.

THE BEST CREWS TREAT ALL DISASTERS AS INCIDENTS AND NONE OF THE INCIDENTS AS DISASTERS.

JOHN C LAURIE

EVERY GAME IN YOUR CAREER IS LIKE A ROAD MAP, BUT YOU STILL NEED A DESTINATION (GOAL) TO GET WHERE YOU WANT TO GO.

WHEN THE GAME BEGINS TO GO WRONG, DON'T YOU GO WRONG.

JOHN C LAURIE

THE BEST OFFICIALS WILL ALWAYS TELL YOU THAT ALL THE "GOOD" THAT HAS COME TO THEM IN OFFICIATING WAS DIFFICULT BEFORE IT BECAME EASY.

FINAL THOUGHTS

AT SOME POINT IN YOUR OFFICIATING CAREER YOU
WILL HAVE A PLAY OR SITUATION IN WHICH YOU WILL
CHOOSE TO PROTECT YOUR REPUTATION OR TO MAKE
THE RIGHT DECISION. YOUR CHOICE AT THE TIME MAY BE
VERY DIFFICULT, BUT THE OFFICIAL WITH A GREAT CAREER
ALWAYS MAKES THE RIGHT DECISION AND, IN THE END,
ENHANCES HIS REPUTATION.

IF YOU ALLOW ANOTHER OFFICIAL, A COACH OR
SUPERVISOR TO PULL YOU DOWN SO LOW THAT YOU
"HATE THEM," YOUR POSITION OF CHARACTER AND
LEADERSHIP HAS SLIPPED BELOW THEIR PERCEIVED LEVEL
IN THE MORE IMPORTANT GAME: <u>LIFE</u>.

John C. Laurie

REF-DECKS

INFORMATION FORM

Thank you for your interest in REF-DEKS. I believe you will find this product invaluable to officials who wish to improve! Regardless of your level of officiating, whether you are in the N.F.L. or a high school J.V. official, these cards will help you develop your philosophy of being a better official individually or as a crew.

N.F.L. officials, Ed Hochuli and Red Cashion (retired), have endorsed this product along with several Divisions I & II college officials and supervisors.

Each set consists of 150 (coated) cards with 300 quotations about officiating.

Dr. John Laurie

Big 8, Big XII Referee (retired)

There are seven (7) REF-DECKS sets:

_____ SET 1 WHAT GOOD OFFICIALS DO
_____ SET 2 BEST CREWS
_____ SET 3 COMMUNICATIONS/COACHES
_____ SET 4 LEADERSHIP
_____ SET 5 ROOKIES & MISTAKES
_____ SET 6 SUPERVISORS/OBSERVERS
_____ SET 7 PREGAME & MECHANICS

johnclaurie@yahoo.com

www.betweenthestripesandmore.com   GOOD OFFICIALS

ONE OF THE BEST WAYS TO DESCRIBE A SUCCESSFUL OFFICIAL IS THAT HE HAS OVERCOME THE FEAR OF MAKING A MISTAKE.

©   JOHN C LAURIE

www.betweenthestripesandmore.com   GOOD OFFICIALS

YOU CAN NEVER TALK YOURSELF OUT OF PROBLEMS THAT YOU HAVE BEHAVED YOURSELF INTO.

©   JOHN C LAURIE

THE BEST CREWS WORK EXTRA HARD TO BE "LUCKIER" THAN OTHER CREWS.

© JOHN C LAURIE

THE BEST OFFICIALS HAVE GIVEN A LOT OF PRIOR THOUGHT WHEN REQUIRED TO MAKE SUDDEN DECISIONS.

© JOHN C LAURIE

THE BEST COMMUNICATORS ON THE CREW KNOW THAT NOT EVERY QUESTION A COACH ASKS REQUIRES AN ANSWER.

© JOHN C LAURIE

COMMUNICATIONS/COACHES

THE MOST EFFECTIVE ANSWER YOU CAN GIVE A COACH IS THE ONE WHICH DESTROYS HIS QUESTION.

© JOHN C LAURIE

LEADERSHIP

A LEADERLESS CREW PROVIDES AN EQUAL OPPORTUNITY FOR EVERYONE TO BE INCOMPETENT.

© JOHN C LAURIE

LEADERSHIP

A GOOD REFEREE IS THE STRAW THAT STIRS THE DRINK.

© JOHN C LAURIE

ROOKIES & MISTAKES

IF YOU WANT TO KNOW HOW FAR AN OFFICIAL IS HEADED UP OR DOWN IN HIS CAREER, STUDY HIS EXCUSES.

© JOHN C LAURIE

ROOKIES & MISTAKES

IF YOUR CIRCLE OF KNOWLEDGE AND YOUR CIRCLE OF EXPERIENCE ARE NOT THE SAME, CONTINUE TO MAKE BOTH LARGER AND CLOSER TO THE SAME SIZE.

© JOHN C LAURIE

SUPERVISORS & OBSERVERS

A SURVEY SHOWS THAT SLENDER REFEREES HAVE MORE GAMES THAN FAT ONES. THE CHUNKY SON OF THE SUPERVISOR MAY BE AN EXCEPTION.

© JOHN C LAURIE

AFTER EACH GAME ASK, "AM I GETTING A LITTLE BETTER OR A LITTLE WORSE?" IF YOUR ANSWER IS THE SAME THREE GAMES IN A ROW, YOU ARE ON YOUR WAY.

© JOHN C LAURIE

IF YOU REALLY WANT TO LEARN FROM YOUR GAME FILM, TRY TRACING THE EFFECTS OF WHAT CAUSED THE PROBLEMS.

© JOHN C LAURIE

FAILING ON EACH DOWN TO COMMUNICATE TO AT LEAST ONE OTHER OFFICIAL THE DOWN/ DISTANCE IS ABOUT THE SAME AS WINKING AT A PRETTY GIRL IN A DARK CLOSET. YOU KNOW WHAT YOU ARE DOING, BUT NO ONE ELSE DOES.

© JOHN C LAURIE

REF-DECKS

ORDER FORM

NAME				
ADDRESS				
SET	SET TITLE	# SETS	PRICE	TOTAL
1	WHAT GOOD OFFICIALS DO		$10.00	
2	BEST CREWS		$10.00	
3	COMMUNICATIONS & COACHES		$10.00	
4	LEADERSHIP		$10.00	
5	ROOKIES & MISTAKES		$10.00	
6	SUPERVISORS		$10.00	
7	PREGAME & MECHANICS		$10.00	
*	1 COMPLETE SET OF 7	_____	$60.00	_____
		TOTAL	SUB TOTAL	_____
	POSTAGE 1 SET -- $7.00		POSTAGE	_____
	POSTAGE: 2 - 6 SETS -- $10.00		TOTAL	
	*SPECIAL: 1 COMPLETE SET OF 7 -- $60.00 + $10.00 POSTAGE			
	MAKE CHECK PAYABLE TO :			
	DR. JOHN LAURIE			
	BOX 23208			
	OVERLAND PARK, KS 66223			
	PHONE: 913 707 6548			
	PERSONAL MAIL			
	6841 W 138TH TERRACE #722			
	OVERLAND PARK, KS 66223			
	REF DECKS WILL BE MAILED WITHIN 7 DAYS OF NOTIFICATION.			